CW00349293

# Time Together

## Prayers for personal devotion and intercession

## Susan Sayers

**kevin mayhew**

# kevin
# mayhew

First published in Great Britain in 1998 by Kevin Mayhew Ltd
Buxhall, Stowmarket, Suffolk IP14 3BW
Tel: +44 (0) 1449 737978  Fax: +44 (0) 1449 737834
E-mail: info@kevinmayhew.com

www.kevinmayhew.com

© Copyright 1998 Susan Sayers

The right of Susan Sayers to be identified as the author of this work
has been asserted by her in accordance with the Copyright, Designs
and Patents Act 1988.

All rights reserved. No part of this publication may be reproduced,
stored in a retrieval system, or transmitted, in any form or by any
means, electronic, mechanical, photocopying, recording, or otherwise,
without the prior written permission of the publisher.

The publishers wish to thank all those who have given their permission
to reproduce copyright material in this publication.

Every effort has been made to trace the owners of copyright material and we hope
that no copyright has been infringed. Pardon is sought and apology made if the
contrary be the case, and a correction will be made in any reprint of this book.

9 8 7 6 5 4 3 2 1 0

ISBN 978 1 84003 157 7
Catalogue No.1500175

Cover design by Melody-Anne Lee
© Image used under licence from Shutterstock Inc.
Edited by Michael Forster
Typeset by Louise Selfe

Printed and bound in Great Britain

# Contents

# Foreword

Relationships deepen through meaningful communication, and our relationship with the living God who created us will only develop and grow if we are in frequent communication with him. Sometimes we need assistance with this, and it may be helpful for us if we can use printed prayers, to express what we want to say and to encourage us in allowing the Spirit of God to pray through us. It may well be that, having begun with a printed prayer, we are able to carry on praying in our own words, pouring out to the God who both loves and listens whatever is on our mind or in our heart.

The only rule for praying is that we are our real selves in God's company. That is what makes our prayers beautiful, as far as God is concerned, so we should never be put off by thinking that 'proper' praying is reserved for the experts who can make their phrases suitably poetic and grammatically correct. In reality, it is our integrity, honesty and humility which matter, and simply our wanting to get closer to God.

This collection of prayers provides material suitable for personal devotion. There are acts of praise and wonder, thanksgiving and love, springing from our ordinary, everyday work and relationships, and the real world we all inhabit. There are expressions of grief and pain, disappointment and confusion, which are just as important to bring to God as the good times and the moments of spiritual uplift. And there are frameworks for intercession which you can use daily as you pray for your church, your community, and the needs of the world.

All the prayers are to be prayed, not recited, taking as much time over them as you like, with as many variations as you wish to make. It is my hope that they will help you draw closer to God as you walk together, talking and listening to one another.

SUSAN SAYERS, 1998

# PART 1

---

## Personal Devotional

# Prayers of Invocation and Approach

Loving God,             *1*
    bless our time together today
    as we talk over memories,
    catch up on news
    and put the world to rights.

It seems no time at all
    since we were students
    sharing our lives' secrets,
    and the kitchen
    and our dreams.

Thank you for our friendship
    over the years
    and all it has given us.


When my mind is         *2*
    fully occupied
    with the business of the day,
    be in my thinking
    and speaking
    and action, O God,
    and make me a channel
    of your loving,
    however busy I am.

3    Lord,
        I may only see each face
        briefly today,
        but I know each face
        is a person loved into being
        by you.

    As our eyes meet,
        as we discuss a product
        or comment on the weather
        may your blessing
        be upon them
        and their loved ones

4    Father, before this meeting
        I still myself
        and remember your presence.

    I lay before you
        the whole agenda
        both written and hidden.

    I lay before you
        each person present.

    Let your kingdom come
        in our discussions
        and in our decisions,
        and let only your will
        be done.

Under the pressure and stress –
The loving God.

Under the tedious repetition –
The loving God.

Under the financial
    and managerial headaches –
The loving God.

Under the crowded schedule
    and rushed decisions –
The loving God.

Under the traffic jams
    and copier failure –
The loving God.

Under the seconds and
    weeks and years –
The loving God.


Lord,
    as I listen and respond
    to the anger and hurt,
    surround this person
    with your reassurance,
    with your understanding,
    with your acceptance,
    until they feel safe
    and of value.

7    Father, will you show me today,
        the gaps to recollect
        your love
        and praise you.

    I want to use those seconds
        and minutes
        instead of filling them up
        with plans for the future
        and regrets for the past.

    Help me to re-establish
        the present
        in my life,
        and your presence
        in my present,
        so I can touch base
        throughout my work
        and know, in my soul's stillness,
        know that you are God.

8    Lord, I thirst for the freedom you offer,
        your perfect freedom
        which shatters the prisons of self and sin,
        and scatters the shadows
        of failure and fear.
    Lord, God of true freedom,
        come, set me free.

Lord, in a world vibrating with action 9
    I have come here to be still.
In a world of tight schedules and deadlines
    I have come to absorb the present.
In a world of limits and frustrations
    I have come to the brink of eternity.
At the still point of this churning world
    I can meet you, the unchanging God,
    and know your peace.


Lord, you alone can 10
    supply my deepest need;
    you alone can satisfy and fulfil.

Come, Holy Spirit of God,
    come and fill me to overflowing.


Out of the darkness and void, 11
    God is creating.
Out of chaos,
    God is bringing order.
Out of the fragments we offer,
    God is creating wholeness.
Into despair,
    God breathes hope.
Into anxiety,
    God breathes peace.
Into deadness,
    God breathes life.

12    Before and after time,
       there is God.
    Where past and future are gathered,
       there is God.
    Beyond the death of the body,
       there is God.
    For you, O Lord, are everlasting,
       faithful for ever and eternally present.
    You are the great 'I AM' and I worship you.

13    Hold me close to you,
       Lord, my God,
       my shepherd.

    A lot of me
       wants to go racing off
       to the thickets and cliffs
       away from your care.

    Hold me close
       and let me know
       your presence
       whispering courage
       and strength
       until the desire to wander away
       wanders away.

Where are you, O God?                    *14*
I search for you
    and long to feel you near,
    but my prayers
    land in the empty air
    and I have to force myself
    to bother
    as I feel nothing.

All I hang on to
    is that feelings
    are not everything,
    and just because this fog
    surrounds me
    does not mean
    that everything has gone.

One thing I have discovered –
    I had not realised before
    how much I delighted
    in your company.


Lord, may your stillness within me,            *15*
    which comes from you and is your indwelling,
    stay with me, calm and refresh me,
    throughout each moment of my living.

16    Fill me again
        with your Spirit, O God.

        Spread through my mind
           until I think your way.

        Wander through my emotions
           and bring them in line
           with the measure of your love.

        Anoint my wounds
           with the balm of your healing.

        Empower my being
           to reflect your beauty
           in the way I live,
           from now onwards
           to the end of my days.

17    Lord God,
        this is an invitation.

        I've been inviting all my loved ones
           to this celebration
           and you are the
           most important guest.

        Bless our festivities
           and all our preparations
           so that our time together
           will be filled with joy
           in your presence.

Holy God,                                            18
   the radiance of your love
   touches my life
   with tenderness
   and warmth.

It stretches over the doubts
   and calms them.

It searches out the misgivings
   and reassures.
It mops up errors,
   binds unravelled relationships
   and pierces prejudice.

Holy God,
   wrap your radiance
   around my life
   until my life
   is hidden in yours.

Welcome, holy God,                                   19
   for I have come to seek you,
   to meet you,
   to worship you.

With the dust of life's journey on my feet,
   and the checklist of daily tasks
   still teeming in my mind,
   I come to settle myself at your feet
   and to honour you above all else.

20    I've been dipping into
          memories, Lord God,
          and thinking
          how much
          the world has changed
          since I was young.

      And many of those
          I knew and loved
          are no longer here.

      It frightens me a little
          to think of the future.

      I can't bear the thought
          of losing the independence
          I have always enjoyed.

      Be with me every step of the way,
          whatever the journey ahead.




21    Great and faithful God,
          it is your nature to accompany me;
          to grieve at my wounding,
          to share in my joy,
          to gather me up when I stumble,
          to calm me when I am afraid,
          to nudge me into action,
          to curb my excesses.

      Through days and lifetimes,
          you are Emmanuel – 'God with us'.

Lord God, I come into your presence.                  22
Deliberately I do this first,
   before the business of the meeting
   and before anything at all is discussed.

Before I speak
   I have come to listen.

Before I make decisions
   I have come to discern your will.

Quieten my heart to hear you, holy God.


When my life becomes overcrowded with importance,   23
   and the diary is full,
   and the weeks are short,
   then get in the way and disturb my routine
   until I remember that you, Lord God,
   are the centre and foundation.

When the troubles and changes dismember my peace,
   and the future intimidates me,
   and the past haunts me,
   then whisper your truth in the core of my being
   until I remember that you, Lord God,
   are almighty and here.

When I become complacent and think I am in control,
   and strangers don't fit,
   and all change is threat,
   then break me apart;
   scatter my assumptions in the gale of your breath;
   teach me to live in the unpredictable freedom
   of your Spirit.

24    Father God, all that I am lies before you,
          my achievements and disappointments,
          my dreams and misgivings,
          my commitments and responsibilities,
          my gifts and weaknesses.

      Take me as I am,
          where I am,
          and make me fully myself,
          strong in your strength and rich with your love,
          as I serve only you,
          the God of my making,
          with heart and mind and spirit
          in all that I think and say and do.

25    Lord God, my maker,
          all powerful and all seeing,
          I worship you.

      Lord God, my redeemer,
          all loving and compassionate,
          I worship you.

      Lord God, my comforter,
          enabling and transforming,
          I worship you.

      Before the beginning,
          and after the end,
          and for ever,
          you are the one, true God,
          and I worship and adore you.

# Prayers for Grace

There is something
    particularly special
    about celebrating together
    with a shared meal –
    the food and drink,
    the conversations,
    the looking after
    one another's needs.

And as we gather
    at the sharing of your feast,
    and you feed us
    and you quench our thirst,
    supplying our needs,
    let the harmony and love among us
    grow and mellow
    in your peace.

*26*

O Lord,
    if I didn't love him so much
    it wouldn't hurt so much.
I could simply shrug my shoulders
    and ignore him.

But as it is
    I do love him – dearly.

So help me to reach out again
    and start the healing.

*27*

28    Jesus, friend of sinners,
        friend of publicans,
        tax collectors and prostitutes,
        friend of outcasts,
        friend of the despised,
        friend of the ineffective and the inadequate,
        friend of prisoners,
        friend of traitors,
        be my friend,
        and give me the grace
        to reach out
        to your other friends
        in an open,
        two-way friendship.

29    O God my parent,
        touch my parenting
        with greater patience
        and deeper love.

    O God my parent,
        season my parenting
        with helpless laughter
        and a sense of wonder.

    O God my parent,
        undergird my parenting
        with hope
        and trust
        and tranquillity.

My God, my parent, dress me          *30*
   in patience and humility
   in righteousness and love.

My God, my parent, feed me
   and quench my thirst
   with your life-giving Spirit.

For I too am a dresser and feeder,
   I too am a quencher of thirst,
   and I know what it is
   to respond to needs out of love.

So, in the trust my child is teaching me,
   I, a parent,
   come to you, my parent God,
   knowing that you will supply
   all my needs.

Lord, it's late          *31*
   and my daughter should be back
   and she isn't back.

I'm probably foolish
   to worry,
   but I do.

I'm probably foolish
   to imagine things,
   but I do.

I ask you to keep her safe
   and protect her from all harm.

32   Loving Father,
         I woke up remembering
         that today is results day,
         and my child
         and thousands of others
         will find out whether or not
         they've achieved the grades they need.

     Whole futures
         will be adjusted today.

     If comforting is in order,
         give me useful words to say.
     If disappointment is taken out on me,
         help me to understand.
     Whatever the result, Lord God,
         use it for good.


33   The end of the holiday, Lord,
         and my daughter is packing
         to go back to university.
     The rucksack bulges
         as the character of her room empties.

     She is my friend
         as well as my child
         and I love her company.

     Accompany her
         in the assignments,
         in the pub,
         and in the shared kitchen.

     And thank you, Lord,
         for her loveliness.

Father, I need your guidance            *34*
   in a difficult situation.
I'm worried about this latest friend
   my son's taken up with.

I can't put my finger
   on the reason,
   but I just know
   I'm wary and concerned.

Please give me discernment
   and your wisdom
   to know when to speak
   and when to hold back
   from speaking,
   when to intervene
   and when to let well alone.

And in all things
   let your will be done.

God of wisdom and power,            *35*
   you alone have the words of eternal life.

I thirst for your goodness,
   and come to you for drink.

I hunger for your righteousness
   and come to you for food.

36    O my Father,
         the painting pots and modelling dough
         were set out fresh on low clean tables,
         and my child clung tighter and tighter,
         mouth thumb-jammed.

     I feel such an ache
         at leaving her there,
         even though I know
         she's fine soon after I've left.

     Loving Father,
         be with our child
         and all the children
         as they play today.

     Be with the leaders and helpers.
     Be in the story time and singing.
     Be in the growing friendships
         and in the tentative building of community.

     Through all the loving care they find
         may they sense your love
         holding them safe as their world grows.


37    Lord, as our love
         for one another grows,
         keep us rooted
         firmly and deeply
         in your unending love.

     And as we each
         grow closer to you,
         draw us closer
         to one another.

Lord, it's his first night                    38
   away from home;
   his first time camping, too.
We've labelled everything,
   and squashed it all into a bag,
   and packed a cake
   and painted his name on plates and mug,
   and helped him stagger with everything
   on to the bus.

So now, Lord,
   be with them all as they travel.
Be at the site when they arrive,
   and in all their activities.
Give them a great time
   with lots of fun
   and help them to get along together.
Then, tired and smelly,
   bring them safely home!

Lord, give me your peace;                    39
   help me to accept the peace you give.
May your peace soak up my thoughts,
   flood my feelings,
   still my body,
   fill this place.
In your peace let me relax, now,
   accepting myself
   and the people I love
   as you are accepting me.
Lord, give me your peace.

40      Father, I need your help
            in the task ahead of me
            today.

        I know there are going to be
            tensions
            and delicate handling
            will be necessary.

        To be honest, I'm scared.
        Scared of messing it all up,
            and leaving people damaged.

        What I pray for
            is a double dose of your
            wise and generous love,
            for your constant guidance
            and enfolding presence.

        Father, your grace is sufficient.


41      God of my making,
            patient and thorough,
            bless the making
            I shall be doing today.

        May I, too,
            be patient and thorough,
            valuing the doing
            as well as the result.

God of wisdom,                                          42
    I need your help.

It is as if I am standing
    at a crossroads,
    with signs pointing
    in different directions
    and I need
    to make a choice.

As I weigh up
    the advantages and disadvantages
    of each direction
    I ask you to guide me
    and cause me to bring to mind
    everything necessary
    to making
    the best decision.


It's not that long, Lord,                               43
    before I retire,
    and I want to talk over with you
    how best to prepare
    and how best to use that time.

Please guide me in all
    the important decisions,
    show me to any doors
    you want me to open,
    and, above all,
    make my life fruitful
    both now and through my retirement.

44    When we are totally at one,
       spent and fulfilled
       in one another,

       your love, O God, pervades us.

    When tempers flare
       and reconciliation is costly,

       your love, O God, restores us.

    When illness and frailty
       disrupt our hopes and plans,

       your love, O God, sustains us.


45    Isn't it strange, Lord,
       how you can spend time
       with someone you love
       and not need to speak,
       necessarily, at all.

    And yet the communication
       is powerful and deep.

    It is as if we are wrapped up
       in a cloth of affection
       woven with colours
       we both enjoy,
       warm to the touch
       but unrestricting –
       like your love to us
       which holds us
       yet enables us to be free.

God of love,  46
   teach me to love
   the way you love.

Teach me the love
   I can promise with my own will;
   the love which
   doesn't rely on feelings;
   the love which is not reliant
   on mutual attraction
   or warm response;

   the love that reaches out
   without demanding
   emotional feedback;
   the love that
   sets self down
   and rolls up its sleeves
   for action.

Lord, I stood at the door  47
   and watched
   this woman, my wife,
   walking down the street
   with our child.

She didn't know I was watching.
They were talking together
   and smiling.
She was beautiful.

I love her so much
   for all that she is to me.

48 Loving God,
    we dedicate ourselves afresh
    to one another
    and to you.

On this, our anniversary,
    we call to mind
    the journey we have travelled together,
    the dark and sunlit places,
    the storms and the havens.

Thank you, Lord God,
    for your loving,
    your faithfulness
    within ours.

Once more we commit ourselves
    to love and to cherish
    within the arch
    of your cherishing.

I am going to miss                                        49
   these people, Lord,
   after spending a week
   on holiday together.

You get so close,
   sharing meals and jokes
   and difficulties
   and worship.

I suppose we have grown
   from a group of individuals
   into a community.

Perhaps we have grown
   into more of a church,
   with mutual concern,
   brotherly and sisterly love.

Let this not be lost
   as we go home, Lord,
   but use it
   for the good of the world.

50    It is good to rest
          and relax
          with a drink
          as muscles sing
          after physical work.

      I remember
          the wholesome
          resting of God
          at the end of
          creation's labour.

      God, make me content
          to sit for a while
          and remember
          that rest is necessary
          and not an optional extra.

Lord God, you have taught me          *51*
   that wherever love is, there you are.

What kind of love is your love?

It is love that forgives
   and then forgives,
   and forgives again.

It is love that rolls up its sleeves
   and gets involved with caring
   and mending and building.

It is love that is quite happy
   to be considered foolish,
   to be considered weak.

It is love that keeps on giving,
   but keeps no accounts;
   that is non-selective
   and unconditional.

This is the nature of your love,
   for this is the nature of you.
   And I thank you.

52  Lord, I thank you
        for the companions you have given me
        and the friendships I enjoy.

    I thank you for those I can laugh
        and cry with,
        those I relax with,
        those I am most comfortable with
        because they accept me
        and like me
        as I am.
    Lord, I am sorry
        for the times I have let my friends down;
        expected too much of them,
        or too little.

    I am sorry
        that sometimes my selfishness
        causes friction and sadness.

    Lord, I ask you
        to bless my friendships
        and fill them
        with your love.

After the turmoil,                               53
  God of peace,
  you bring me to this
  quiet haven for a while.

I am so grateful
  for a breathing space,
  for respite,
  for refreshment.

I remember the words
  of the psalm –
  'He leads me beside still waters' –
  and know them to be true.

The peace is filtering
  deeper and deeper
  into my being
  and in the tranquillity
  I know
  that you are God.

We have made our vows                        54
  in your presence, Lord,
  and laid down the single life
  to become this new creation –
  a married couple.

We invited you
  to the wedding, Lord,
  and now we invite you
  to the entire marriage,
  and all that distance
  we shall be travelling together.

# Prayers of Joy, Praise and Thanksgiving

55    Father, I want to thank you
         for the extraordinary
         outpouring of love
         I have experienced
         through being ill.
      People are so kind!

      It isn't just the cards
         and flowers
         (which really helped
         and lifted my spirits)
         but it's also the expression
         in their eyes,
         the praying for me
         when I couldn't pray myself;
         the being there
         and standing alongside.

      It was your love
         I was experiencing,
         wasn't it, Lord?
      Your amazing love!

Isn't it strange, Lord,                56
   how we sometimes set out
   thinking we're doing the good deed
   and end up being the receivers.

To be honest,
   I wasn't looking forward
   to visiting this elderly neighbour
   and I did it feeling noble.

How wrong can you be!
I really look forward to those visits now.

She ensures that I sit down
   and I relax and listen
   to her wonderful stories
   from a completely different world
   I was born too late to inhabit.

It's quality time
   and I really am thankful
   for our friendship.


Thank you, my loving God,          57
   for my baby's first gift to me today:
   a half-chewed rusk,
   lovingly thrust into mouth.

Bless my baby's developing generosity
   and thank you for making us all
   in the likeness of your
   loving, generous nature.

58 Thank you, Lord,
  for that phone call from my friend.
Just when I needed
  cheering up;
  she rang
  and cheered me up.

 Just when I needed
  to see the funny side of things
  she showed it to me
  and we ended up laughing.

 What a gift!
 Thank you, my Lord.

59 Two friends
  sharing a drink together
  after work.

 A joke or two.
 A wry telling of the day's woe.

 The tensions slide away
  and it truly feels like
  re-creation, my Lord.

 You were right,
  we do need one another.

 I praise and thank you
  for your wholesome provision
  of mutual comfort and renewing
  in a good friendship.

Lord, I want to thank you                              60
   for my doggy friend here,
   grinning away in his doggy way,
   tail thrashing!

What would a muddy walk
   be without him?
What would coming home be
   without his wet and lavish welcome?

It's a very special
   doggy/human friendship
   we enjoy!

If I were you, my Lord,                                61
   I would probably have
   given up on me, by now.

Thank you, my Lord,
   for forgiving
   again and again and again.

Thank you for using
   each tangled mess
   I present you with,
   in some strange way,
   for good.

You are indeed
   faithful
   and of great mercy.

62    Lord, our God,
        our parent and our friend,
        as our child takes his first unsteady steps
        and we smile and encourage him,
        and scoop him up when he falls
        and set him down to try again,
        we want to share our joy with you,
        and thank you
        for the way you scoop *us* up
        when we fall,
        and set us down
        to try again.

63    The head strains to be born,
        the shoulders follow
        and suddenly I am a Dad.

There's my lovely wife – a Mother
        and here's the child of our love.
You've done a good job, Lord God,
        an incredible job.

A miracle!

You've made us into a family,
        wrapped up in love, and crying together
        with joy and relief and utter exhaustion.

Father,                                    64
    I've been watching my children
    spend quality time with snails.

And I'm beginning to see
    why you advised us
    to become like young children.

I'm not sure that I give
    so much full attention
    to my friends.

So often, we're thinking ahead,
    or remembering something,
    or waiting to say our bit.

Thank you
    for the example of our children
    who live in the present
    and value it.

65    Look, Lord,
    isn't this an incredible ship
    they've made out of junk!

    It's true, we are indeed
      made in your image –
      creative and constructive.

    Children are so good
      at using whatever is available.

    Thank you for using them
      to show me
      that there's nothing,
      no one,
      and no situation
      that can't be used for good.


66    Do you know, Lord,
    I was wondering if going on holiday
    was really worth the effort.
    And now I can see that it was.

    Thank you so much for
      bringing us safely
      to such a beautiful place.
    We can sit here and watch
      our children's store of good memories
      building as they play.

    Life is good! Thank you!

Well, my Lord,                                              67
    here it is –
    the five-metre swimming badge,
    and you and I both know
    the struggle and determination
    that it celebrates!

You know, my Lord,
    I'm not at all sure
    that I would have coped
    if I had such difficulties.

Thank you for all
    your encouragement
    at every painstaking stage
    of development.
    Thank you for helping us
    not to give up.
    And most of all,
    thank you for that huge
    beaming smile on her face
    as she reached the side of the pool.
It said it all!




All powerful Lord,                                         68
    I honour you.
Lord of the universe and all creation,
    I offer you my praise.
Lord of all time and distance,
    I worship and adore you.

69    Dear Lord,
        I've spent years
        trying to get my son
        to keep his room
        in some kind of order.

      And now here I am
        ridiculously sobbing to myself
        because it is so tidy!

      I know I'm a fool
        and I'll get on with things in a minute.

      But, Lord, this immaculate,
        unlived-in room reminds me sharply
        of how dearly I love him
        and how much I miss him
        while he's away.

      Thank you for the privilege
        of his company
        for the last eighteen years!


70    Thank you, Lord,
        for the helpless laughter
        that overtook us all
        in the staff room today.

      It was exactly what we needed
        to counteract the stress
        at the end of a gruelling term.

      Thank you for each one
        of my colleagues
        and the work they do.

Thank you for the privilege                                            71
    of meeting
    the people I have worked with today.

Thank you for their
    good-natured humanness,
    their earnestness and cheerfulness.

Thank you for their
    sense of humour and friendship;
    for difficulties grasped with
    determination to win.

Behind every face
    a landscape of struggle and
    hope, fear and resignation.

Thank you for all
    they have given and taught
    through being themselves.

Lord God, source of life,                                              72
    I rejoice that through the power
    of your love I am alive;
    a breathing, thinking, feeling creature,
    made in your likeness
    and for your glory.

Lord God, source of life,
    recognising that my life exists
    through your desire
    I thank you and praise you
    and glorify you.

73     Lord, how can I ever thank you
           for all that you are
           and all that you have done?

       I praise you for the wonder
           of all life that grows;
           for pattern and order,
           the complex and the simple.

       The whole universe reflects your glory
           from the wideness of space
           to the detail of cells;
           from the rainbow to the raindrop,
           from the frog to the whale;
           the whole universe reflects your glory
           and I worship you.


74     It was with joy that Mary sang;
           it was news of great joy
           which the angels proclaimed.

       With joy, the shepherd finds his lost sheep,
           the woman her lost coin,
           the ploughman his hidden treasure.

       Lord, your kingdom
           is a kingdom of joy –
           a deep delight which lasts for ever
           and is for ever renewed;
           a freshwater spring
           that never runs dry.
       Lord, give me this joy.

Lord, I thank you that time and time again         *75*
   you encourage me on my journey.
Whenever weakness overtakes me,
   whenever your will seems blocked,
   whenever the next step looks treacherous,
   whenever I reach the limits of my resources;
   then you encourage and strengthen my resolve,
   you show me that with you all things are possible,
   you support me during the difficult moves,
   and provide for my every need.
O Lord my God,
   without your encouragement
   I would so often give up;
   I thank you for empowering me
   to work for the coming of your kingdom.

Lord, I praise you         *76*
that in order to save me
   you accepted the limitations of humanity;
in order to set me free
   you accepted death by crucifixion;
in order to redeem me
   you accepted the need
   to pay the price for sin
   in full,
   and without condition.
O Lord my God,
   I thank you and adore you.

77    Lord, I owe my entire existence
       to your constant love for me.
In you alone, all creatures
       live and move and have their being.
Our genetic inheritance,
       our genetic functioning;
       all is designed and sustained
       by the mastery of your hands
       and the power of your love.

Not only in this body,
       but throughout the whole of creation,
       there is order and pattern,
       structure and design,
       balance and beauty.

O Lord, my God,
       how excellent are your ways.
Let everything that has breath
       praise you!

Loving God,                                          *78*
  your caring
  over the last few months
  has amazed me.

I had heard it said
  that when one door closed
  another opened;
  but I was sceptical.

And that door
  was slammed so suddenly.

The strange thing is,
  I had hardly noticed
  the new door opening
  until I was halfway through.

Thank you,
  my loving God,
  for your providing.

79  O my God,
       I feel so excited
       and I want to share it
       with you.

    What I thought was
       completely beyond reach
       I have achieved.

    Now that I've passed,
       all the hard work
       seems worthwhile.

    But I can hardly believe
       it's really happened.

    Thank you, my God,
       for all your love and support.

    What next?

I realised today, Lord,                                    *80*
   that I've moved on
   a generation.

It happened so gradually
   that I hardly noticed,
   and it feels a bit like
   getting used to new shoes.

As I get older,
   it is comforting to know
   that you love all of me,
   and your love is not in the least affected
   by my age or looks
   or health or capabilities.


As the planet turns, O God,                                 *81*
   new voices wake to sing your praise
   and the earth is circled
   with an unending chain of prayer.

Blessed are you, unchanging God,
   who already were in the beginning,
   who are, at this moment,
   and who will be for ever.

# Prayers of Trust and Hope

82    Being your friend, Jesus,
      certainly doesn't make
      for a dull life.

    Just when I think
      I'm getting the hang of things,
      you call me on
      to a new situation.

    Just when I'm
      beginning to think
      you've gone without me,
      I find you at my side.

    Lead on, my friend:
      this journey
      may not be club class travel
      but it's the only way
      for me!

83    O God, my God,
      you are the source of all things,
      you are the redeemer of all things,
      you are the essence of all things.

    In you I hope.
    In you I become.
    In you I live.

Loving God,                                                  84
   I cannot bear the thought
   of my children being damaged
   by my mishandling
   or lack of parenting skill.

I know that, realistically,
   I'm bound to mess things up
   from time to time,
   and I know that children
   are remarkably resilient.

But what if their lives were to become
   crippled or distorted
   because of my mistakes?

I ask your indwelling, loving God,
   so that any potential damage
   becomes instead
   an opportunity for growth.

And I ask for you to calm my fears
   and remind me, regularly,
   that love covers a multitude of sins.

Lord, speak to our baby of peace in the pain,      85
   of hope in the turmoil, of love all around.

Speak to our baby
   whose body has ripened for birth
   and safeguard this journey to light.

86      Father, I pray
            for my children's future
            and, if they are to marry,
            for their partners.

        Bless their growing
            and their physical, mental,
            emotional and spiritual development,
            wherever they may be,
            so that good foundations are laid
            for a fulfilling and lasting marriage.

        And I pray for all those
            my children will be close to
            throughout their lives,
            their friends and colleagues,
            their children and grandchildren.

        Father, in all the future
            let your will be done.

87      Lord, to whom else could I go?
        You alone have the words of eternal life.
        I ask you to open my mind to
            greater possibilities;
            to push back the margins
            of my understanding;
            that I may think your thoughts
            and look with your eyes.
        O Lord my God, to whom else could I go?
        You alone have the words of eternal life.

Repairing can't be rushed,                    88
    can it, my Lord?
It can't be forced.

The foundation work
    and hidden making-good
    are vital.

As I scrape away
    at layers of painted
    woodchip
    and crumbling plaster,
    I begin to understand
    the redemptive work
    of your love –
    thorough, laborious,
    demanding,
    and the only way to make good.


Lord, when your people are still far off,    89
    you see us and run to welcome us.
When we panic and start sinking,
    your arms are quick to hold us up.
When we get lost and wander aimlessly,
    you never stop searching
    until you have found us.

And so I come now to worship you
    for you are the Good Shepherd,
    and I one of the sheep of your pasture.

Lord, I receive your love.

90   Lord God, in the confusion and noise of living
         you listen and hear my secret thoughts.
     Among the endless battering of words,
         you listen and hear my unspoken longings.
     Through the barrage of anger and misunderstanding,
         you listen and hear the pain that I hide.

     You hear the grieving of those that are mourning,
         the joy of lovers and friends,
         the cheep of each sparrow in danger,
         the bleat of each lamb who is lost.

     In my threats,
         you hear my fear;
     in my jealousy,
         you hear my cry to be valued;
     in my lack of forgiveness,
         you hear my need to be forgiven.

     And so I can come before you
         in honesty and simplicity,
         without pretence or exaggeration,
         for you have heard me already
         and know my needs, longings and fears,
         and I can trust you with everything,
         even my very self.


91   Great Spirit of God,
         abundant and unique,
         boundless and intimate,
     you are my God
         and I am your child.
     You are my shepherd,
         and I am a sheep of your pasture.

Lord, not only do you lead the way:          92
   you are the way.
Through you,
   and in you, is the Way of love;
   through you, and in you, is the Way of life.

Lord, you have always led your people,
   and travelled with them.

You called Abraham from the city to the desert.
Jacob discovered your closeness in his
   loneliness as he fled from Esau.
As Moses and the people of Israel
   travelled in the wilderness,
   you went before them always:
   a pillar of cloud by day
   and at night a pillar of fire.

No darkness is too dark for you;
   no depth or height is beyond your reach.
You are there at my going out and my coming in
   from this time forward for evermore.

Lord, I give you thanks and praise,          93
   for in spite of my weakness
   and the poverty of my being,
   you are always faithful in your love for me.

Though I let you down
   and turn from your presence,
   yet you never forget me,
   never give up on me, never stop loving me.

94    Lord, in my weakness
        I come to you for strength.
   In my blindness,
        I come to you for sight.
   In my desire for good to be accomplished,
        I come to you,
        the source of all goodness.
   In my longing for the coming of the kingdom,
        I approach you, the King of kings.

   Lord my God,
        your light dispels all darkness,
        your springs make deserts blossom;
        the warmth of your love
        melts what is frozen,
        restores what is lost,
        refreshes what is weary.

   In you, Lord God, there is always hope,
        because you have overcome sin and death,
        and opened the gates of heaven.


95    Lord, I lay at your feet
        all that I am,
        all that I have been,
        and all that I could become.

   Because I can come to you honestly,
        and because I can trust you
        not to reject me,
        I have come to confide in you
        my secret pains and sorrows,
        my nagging doubts and regrets,
        and my deepest fears.

Into your hands, O Lord,
   I commit my spirit.

I commit the good
   I have tried to do,
   and the good I have avoided.

I commit my heart
   with all the love
   that you find inside.

I commit my living
   and my dying
   into your safekeeping
   for ever.

96

How odd it is, Lord,
   that so often
   it's the times we feel
   we're getting nowhere
   that turn out to be
   times of surging growth!

And I suspect
   the reverse is true as well.

Next time I'm hanging on
   for dear life, Lord,
   remind me
   that spiritual progress
   can go on in tunnels
   as well as in open country.

97

98    So, Lord, it is time
       to adjust
       to these restrictions
       my body is imposing
       as it ages.

I've been angry with it
       long enough.

Help me, Lord,
       to learn to be fond of it again,
       and look at the things
       I can still do,
       instead of the things I can't.


99    Shadows lengthen,
       darkness thickens,
       the lights are lit
       and the day I have lived through comes to an end.

I worship you, my God,
       who separated light from darkness.

Hallowed be your name.

I worship you, my God,
       who ordered the birth of stars.

Hallowed be your name.

I worship you, my God,
       who watches over me, unsleeping,
       night and day.

Hallowed be your name.

# Prayers of Repentance and Forgiveness

Lord my God, *100*
  I come to you in sadness
  knowing that I have let
  my good friend down.

I know she is hurt
  and upset by my absence
  and I have no excuse.
Being busy
  really is no excuse.

Perhaps I should look at my life,
  at my priorities.
If I haven't enough time
  for friends when they need me,
  what are my values?

Help me sort this important
  question out, Lord God.
Show me what needs to change.

101     Forgive me, Lord,
            I did far too much talking
            and missed out on the listening.

        I think I was scared
            of there being long silences
            so I filled the gaps.

        But there need to be a few spaces;
            time to think.

        Give me the courage next time
            to welcome the patches of silence
            for our friendship
            to take root in
            and grow.


102     When we were laughing
            and joking together
            it just felt like a good time.

        But now, Lord,
            thinking it over,
            I can see that it got out of hand
            and more than a bit unkind.
        Perhaps it's not surprising,
            after all,
            that one of them
            left, upset.

        I'm sorry.
        I want to put things right.
        Give me the opportunity
            to apologise
            and sort it out.

What should I have done,                    *103*
   O Lord?
What should I have said?

Can you give me an action replay
   in slow motion
   and take me through it
   to help me understand
   how it turned
   from a light-hearted discussion
   into such a fierce and heated
   argument?
You, after all,
   know both of us.

I want to learn from this.
I want to know
   how to put things right.
So will you teach me?

The jokes today                    *104*
   were crude in the extreme
   and I sat there
   pretending to laugh
   and feeling sick inside
   and ashamed
   because I hadn't the guts
   to speak out
   and say that I found it
   offensive.

O God, my God,
   give me courage
   to stand up for what I believe,
   to speak out when necessary
   and face the pitying stares.

105    Merciful God,
      have mercy on this world.
My child saw the news today
    and looked me straight in the eye –
'But why are they killing each other?'

And I felt suddenly
    ashamed, Lord God,
    of the way we adults live,
    of the destructive decisions,
    of the corruption
    and injustice.

It is true,
    we are like sheep
    without a shepherd.

O God, have mercy on this world.


106    Father, forgive me,
      and help me to put things right.

It was a stupid decision
    I made this week
    and I should have known better,
    and I should have
    thought it all over carefully.

And now there is much repairing to do
    in broken materials and
    broken trust.

Bless the rebuilding,
    my Lord and redeemer,
    and let some good
    emerge from the damage.

Jesus, you call people to you      *107*
   from different places,
   and from different backgrounds,
   to unite us in your love.

Lord, I acknowledge my part
   in the divisions of your world and church.
Between the ideals and the pressures
   there is compromise;
between the dreams and the realities
   there are frustrations;
between the belief and the expression
   there is misunderstanding and conflict.

So, Lord, I ask you to unite
   your world and your church.
To whom else could we go?
You alone have the words of eternal life!

Give us all grace to centre our lives on you,
   melt our divisions, and make us one.


Lord, you are so patient with me;      *108*
so often I lag behind your will,
   or race ahead with my own plans;
so often I do the right things
   for the wrong reasons
   and fail to obey your will.

Yet time and again you search me out
   and find me,
time and again you forgive me
   and bring me safely home.

Most patient Saviour,
   I love you and adore you.

109   It's been a long time
          since I spoke with you.
      Do you remember
          who I am?
      So much else
          has crowded in
          that I haven't found time
          to pray.

      The trouble is,
          as I've started to realise,
          I needed you
          all the time I crowded you out.

      It felt awkward
          and embarrassing
          to make that first move back,
          but already
          I sense the beauty of your peace
          washing around me.

      Forgive me, Lord.
      Your welcome
          fills my eyes
          and my heart with tears.

The journey through life                                          *110*
    goes round in circles
    sometimes, Lord.

Same old sins,
    same old weaknesses
    to overcome.

But perhaps
    it's more of a spiral
    than a circle.

Still revisiting
    the same places, it's true,
    but travelling deeper,
    edging down
    into your heart.


Lord God, maker and saviour,                                      *111*
I have examined my conscience
    in the light of your presence.
I have brought to mind things that cause you pain,
    that burden my life with guilt and regret.
I confess to you that I have sinned against your love,
    in what I have done and in what I have failed to do.
I am sorry for the grief I have caused you,
    and the pain I have caused your children.
More than anything, I long to be forgiven,
    for my sin to be hurled into the depths of the sea.
I long for a fresh start, and the opportunity
    to show you my love
    in the way that I live my life.

# Prayers of Faith
# and Commitment

112    Lord God,
        you have adopted us as your children
        and we have adopted this child.

To us is given
    the caring
    the nurturing
    the parenting
    of a human being,
    and he sleeps contentedly,
    trusting us.

Parent this child
    through our parenting, Lord God.

Teach us and guide us
    each day.

O God,                                                                113
   I don't always know
   what to do for the best.

It's keeping the right balance
   that I find so hard.

Help me to keep your
   principles and values
   central in my thinking:

'Act justly,
   love with mercy,
   walk humbly with your God.'

So that when those hard decisions
   have to be made
   I can use your love
   as a measuring stick
   and be alert
   to your beckoning
   wherever it leads.


Lord, in the garden of Gethsemane,                                    114
   you asked your friends
   to watch and pray.
In agony of spirit you prayed,
   knowing the terrible ordeal that was before you:
   knowing the hate in the eyes
   of those who wanted you dead;
   knowing the vulnerability of love.

Lord, give me grace
   to watch and wait with you.

115    Lord, I can hardly believe
        that our youngest is leaving
        the Primary School
        at the end of this term.

        Last parents' evening, last assembly,
        last damp-eyed concert
        and suddenly, the end of an era.

        Memories of pre-eleven
        crowd nostalgically into my mind.

        And yes, Lord, I know
        they have to move on
        and I don't want
        to hold on to their childhood for ever.

        But it makes me realise
        how quickly the years pass.

        Teach me to be better
        at cherishing the present
        while it's here,
        and bless our growing family.

116    Lord, send me out into the day
        filled with your Spirit.

        Equip me to do
        whatever you have in mind
        wherever I go
        and whoever I meet.

Thank you, Jesus,
   for enabling me
   to find the fault
   and put it right.

It occurs to me
   that you are in
   my line of business.

I remember the leper
   who said
   'If you want to, you can
   make me clean',
   and you answered
   that of course you *did* want to,
   and you healed him.
Well, I'm bringing myself
   for an MOT and running repairs.
I'd like you to start work on me
   right away.

*117*

I'm approaching my birthday –
   one of those significant ones –
   and I thought I'd put some time aside
   to think things over
   in your company, Lord.

I want to face questions
   like, 'What have I done
   with my life so far?'
   and, 'Where do I need things
   to be different?'

So shall we face them together?

*118*

119    So, my Lord,
        they have offered me
        promotion!
    Thank you for this new opportunity.
    I want to do something now,
        before I do anything else,
        and that is to dedicate myself
        and all that this new post entails
        entirely and completely to you.

    Guide me in ways of
        right living and
        responsible management.

    Keep my ears from
        deafness to your will,
        my eyes from blindness,
        my feet from walking ahead of you
        or dragging behind.

    Lord of my past, my present and my future,
        I desire to serve you with all
        my heart.


120    O God, lead me on
        from where I am
        to where you
        would have me be.

    Give me the patience
        to accept the bits
        I'd rather do without,
        and courage to move
        when you beckon.

But I'm not qualified.                          *121*

– I will train you.

But I haven't got the time.

– I didn't say, 'As well as',
I said 'instead of'.

But I like what I'm doing already.

– Good!

So why can't I carry on as I am?

– Silence.

All right. You win!


Lord, I live in the middle                      *122*
    of your remarkable creation;
    all around there is evidence
    of your power, your glory,
    your wisdom and your love.
And yet you came to live among your people
    as one who serves.
Instead of lording it over me,
    you stand patiently at the door and knock.
Instead of imposing your presence on me,
    you wait to be invited.
So now I invite you, Lord:
    come to me; abide with me for ever.

123   Years ago, my God, life seemed
      a lengthy, lasting affair.

But suddenly, it's all
      a lot shorter,
      rushing past at breakneck speed,
      and I'm scared
      of it going to waste.

Not that I want
      to cram it to breaking point.

It's more a case of
      making some progress
      in things like wisdom,
      or conquering my weaknesses
      or just loving a bit more rigorously.

Take the rest of my lifetime,
      God of my making,
      and let your will
      be done in me.

124   I come to you, the one, true, living God,
      with my hands empty and open,
      my heart attentive,
      and my spirit willing.

I come to you,
      thirsting for all that is right
      and loving and good;
      hungering to understand you more,
      ready to do your will.

# Prayers in Time
# of Trouble

It hurts to be let down                    *125*
    by your friends,
    doesn't it, Lord.

The more you trusted them
    the worse it feels.

My gut reaction
    is never
    to trust anyone
    ever again.

I'll tell you another thing, though –
    I've never valued your faithfulness
    so much as I do now.


God of compassion,                        *126*
    reach deep
    into the pain
    of this little one
    and bring your comfort.
Bring ease of pain. Bring sleep.

Enable the doctors and nursing staff
    in their healing work
    and surround this little one's cot
    with reassurance
    and peace.

127   What do you think, Jesus:
          is this a valuable friendship
          or is it the beginning
          of a dangerous relationship?

      I suppose the fact that I'm asking
          says it all –
          there must be something
          that makes me uneasy,
          even though nothing explicit
          has ever been said.

      Protect us from evil, O God,
          and lead us not into temptation.

      Remind me of all my family
          whom I love and hold so dear.

      And thank you
          for showing me the warning lights
          in time to avoid the danger.


128   The love you weave around us,
          loving Lord,
          is so sustaining and strong
          and helps us to bear
          what otherwise
          would be beyond our bearing.

      I could not pray as I struggled for life
          but was aware of the
          love and prayers of many
          good and faithful friends
          upholding me
          with that network of your love.

O God,                                        *129*
   I don't think I can stand
   another battle of wills today!

Yes, I know
   it's perfectly healthy
   for two-year-olds to have tantrums.
Yes, I know
   it proves she has a healthy
   strong character.
And yes, I know
   you're supposed to avoid confrontation
   as much as you can.

But it's been a bad day
   and she's tired and I'm tired,
   and it's getting to me
   at about the point of nine
   on a one to ten scale.

Thank you for listening.

Yes, I'll take her out for a walk.
Good idea. Thank you.

My God, watch over                            *130*
   this sleeping child of mine.
His breathing is clogged with cold,
   but at least he is sleeping at last.

Give him rest and refreshing;
   give him comfort and healing,
   because you and I
   both love him.

131    I am numb with grief,
      O God,
      wept dry,
      drained and hollow.

And in the terrible emptiness,
      once filled with the
      oh so lively presence
      of our child,
      screams the unanswerable
      'Why?'

Give me no reasons,
      O God.
Give me only the grace
      to exist through this
      raw and aching pain
      you know so well.

132    Crucified, rejected Christ,
      continuing your work of love
      through all the insults, spitting and scorn,
I offer you the desolation
      and rejection
      that fills my heart
      as the impact of this
      unexpected redundancy
      slams into me
      and all the assumed security
      shatters at my feet.

Take it all
      and weave something of value
      from this heap of broken pieces.

When I woke up this morning        *133*
   I had that sinking feeling
   as I remembered the task
   I had to do today.

You know, Lord,
   how I have been putting it off
   and finding all kinds of other things
   that really must be done instead.

And now I can no longer put it off
   and today is the day.

You know, my Lord,
   what makes me dread it.
You know all my weaknesses and fears.

So it is for encouragement
   and support
   that I pray,
   for you to love me through
   from start to completion.

134   My Lord God,
    you have told us to trust
    and not be anxious.

That is not easy
    when business is struggling
    and bills need paying
    and the financial future
    looks like a dark pit.

I can feel in the tightness
    of muscles in stomach and neck
    that I am constantly worried and tense.
Please help.

Remind me of your promises
    and give me the grace to trust you.
Provide what is needed,
    reassure me when I doubt,
    and use the hard times
    to teach me more of your loving.

Lord,                                                    *135*
   sometimes I feel as if
   I am being pulled
   in all directions at once.

And there I am,
   in the middle,
   holding things together
   and keeping
   communications channels
   open at all costs.

It is then that I realise that
   it is being rooted in you
   that prevents me from snapping.

You are indeed
   the source of my strength
   and my strong foundation!


Lord, you know me better                                 *136*
   than I know myself.
You understand me better
   than I understand myself.

Like a parent,
   watching a child's first steps,
   you are there ready to pick me up
   when I fall down.

As my brother, you have known
   the cruellest temptation.

As my Saviour, you have power
   to break my chains of sin.

137  You are wonderful, holy God,
       the way you provide
       exactly what we need.

     Just when I wonder
       why I am even bothering
       to carry out this work,
       and exhaustion numbs
       the space between my eyes,
       you give me a reason
       in an image or a smile,
       or a need or a look,
       and I suddenly know
       that you haven't forgotten
       and you know my need
       and affirm without fuss
       but like a quiet word
       in my ear.


138  To tell you the truth, my Lord,
       I hardly dare think
       of the years stretching ahead
       and me, trapped in this job I hate.

     You know the reasons I'm here
       and why I have to stay.
     Every morning I try
       to be positive about it all,
       but I don't want to hide from the truth.

     Walk with me in this dark place.
     Enable me to make the best of it.

     And Lord, if it is possible –
       *when* it is possible –
       could you set me free?

My God, my God, my God,    *139*
   I lay before you
   yet another letter
   of rejection;
   yet another impersonal
   computer printout
   to file under 'dashed hopes'.

What is your will
   for me, O God?

I started out positive,
   but I have to admit
   that the positives
   are wearing thin,
   as unemployment
   settles into an undesired normality,
   whispering lessened value
   and hopelessness.

Hear my cry, O God,
   and answer me,
   because, to be honest,
   I am brought very low.

*140*    I want to thank you,
        Lord God of my hope,
        for rescuing me from despair.

It is true
    that you haul us
    out of swampy ground
    and set our feet on a rock.

I was sinking,
    and close to giving up.
Too many sorrows,
    too much pain
    and utter weariness
    engulfed me.

And there were the strong arms
    of your reassuring presence;
    there was the practical help
    through the hands of your friends.

Extraordinary as it may seem,
    I feel quite different.

Safe.

I would be a liar, Lord,                    *141*
   if I pretended all was well.

And there's no fooling you,
   I know.

So let's be honest about this –
   the situation I am in
   hurts like hell.

I can't see anything
   good in it at all.

All I know is that
   you are a good God –
   the Good God –
   and I offer you
   these broken fragments of praise.


I realise we all have to die.                    *142*

It's not so much
   the dying I dread, Lord,
   it's the last stages of the journey.

It's the leave-taking,
   the ebbing of life,
   the body fighting to live.

These things unnerve me.

Loving God,
   calm my fears
   and give me the courage
   to face this final journey
   into new life.

143   It is difficult not to feel hurt
          when you have been passed over
          and dismissed.

I know, Lord,
     that it's probably
     very good for my humility,
     and perhaps it draws attention
     to some empire-building
     which needs to be checked.

But it still hurts.
Please help me to forgive,
     leaving no trace of resentment.

Help me to grow from this,
     and welcome it as
     a means of becoming
     closer to you.

# PART 2

World, Church and People

# God Our Creator and Redeemer

## *We depend on God*

I pray in humility to you, O God,     *144*
  who creates and sustains all things,
  that your glory may be shown in all creation.

I bring before you the world's leaders
  and their governments,
  and all in influential positions;
  that they may make good use
  of their power,
  and aim to serve
  the needs of others.

I remember the disabled,
  the mentally and physically disadvantaged,
  and those whose bodies or minds
  have been damaged
  through accidents or violence,
  that they may know the calm and peace of Christ.

Bless all who depend on me,
  and those upon whom I rely,
  that we may care for each other
  with kindness and friendship,
  knowing that we are all
  brothers and sisters before you.
This I ask, for your name's sake.

## A world of inequality and indifference

145    Loving heavenly Father,
          you hold all creation in your care
          and your power is sufficient for all our needs.
       Give grace to me, and your whole church,
          that we may truly serve the world,
          and proclaim your love
          not only by word but also through action.

       I pray for the world
          with its areas of luxury and deprivation;
          that as people become more aware
          of the problems,
          we may be guided and inspired
          to solve them,
          and as technology brings us closer,
          we may grow in mutual respect
          and understanding.

       Pour out your love
          on the unnoticed, the unloved,
          those whose lives
          are plagued with poverty and disease;
          the homeless and the refugees.

       Give your grace to all families of every nationality;
          that children may be nurtured
          in love and security,
          and homes may be places
          of peace and joy,
          for Jesus Christ's sake.

## Entrust the world to God

Lord, you have promised to hear my prayer,       *146*
   and you are always true to your word.

So I pray in confidence
   for the world-wide Christian family;
   that it may offer hope
   to the despairing,
   peace to the distressed,
   fulfilment to those who seek,
   and refreshment to the weary.

I pray for this shrinking world
   and those whose authority can affect it
   for good or ill;
   that we may all learn to trust
   and forgive each other
   more readily.

Show your compassion
   to those who are chronically ill;
   and those who are approaching death;
   that they may know the peace of Christ
   which extends even through death itself.

Bless my family, and grant
   that we may learn to trust more in you
   than in ourselves,
   and be alert to your guidance each day.
As we learn to trust more in your love,
   may we grow to be more like Christ
   and reflect the radiance of his love;
   through the same Jesus Christ my Lord.

## *Jesus is Lord of heaven and earth*

147    Lord Jesus Christ,
      you are my hope of redemption.
  May the knowledge of you,
      and your Father's love
      be spread through the world.

  So many different cultures and races
      make up creation;
  Help us all to learn from one another,
      until God's kingdom is established on earth.

  Look kindly, Lord Christ,
      on the casualties of materialistic,
      unjust or corrupt society;
      that, in your light people may recognise needs
      and have the courage to act.

  I hold in the light of your love
      all those I know,
      and the circle of lives linked to each one
      at home and at work;
      that they may become channels of your peace
      and your redemptive love.

  Lord Jesus, accept my prayers
      and those of all faithful people;
      fit us for heaven,
      to live with you for ever.

## God redeems his creation

God my Father,                                         *148*
   the earth is rich with your blessing;
   we come to pray to you now.
Let your will be accomplished
   in every life and every situation;
   that Christians may become
   increasingly receptive
   and ready to act as channels
   of your redeeming grace,
   and the world may be drawn
   into your deep, abiding love.

Remember all those who are physically
   or mentally disadvantaged in any way,
   and those who care for them.
Give me greater acceptance of others
   who look, speak or behave
   differently from myself.
Make me more aware
   of the privileges and responsibilities
   of being your child.
I ask this through Jesus Christ my Lord.

## *God gives meaning to creation*

149    Lord, I remember with gratitude
           all that you have done for me;
           I bring to your love the daily work
           of each member of Christ's body:
           that in constant prayer
           we may learn your will
           and your way of doing things,
           until we work exclusively for your glory.

       I bring to your love the mistakes,
           short-sightedness and arrogance of the world;
           that in Christ we may learn
           to respect one another
           and the treasures of the planet we inhabit.

       I bring to your love
           the wounded and the afraid,
           the despairing and the rejected,
           that they may find Christ
           suffering alongside them
           and allow him to restore them to full life.

       I bring to your love my busy concern
           with unimportant things;
           that in spending more time in Christ's company
           I may learn to act and react
           with the character of Jesus.
       Hear the prayers I offer,
           and use me, body, mind and spirit,
           in establishing your kingdom.
       In the name of Jesus I pray.

## Christ, the hope of creation

Lord Christ, you have promised to return;        *150*
    I pray in your spirit that in my Christian life
    I may never become static
    but flow constantly forward
    in the direction you want me to go,
    true to your teaching,
    in unswerving loyalty to you,
    and undistracted by worldly values.

Help us to tend
    and care for the world;
    that its food and riches may be shared
    and wisely used,
    and its resources safely,
    thoughtfully and effectively deployed.

May all who are ill, injured or distressed
    be touched by your healing hand, Jesus,
    and be made whole,
    comforted by your presence.

Make me more watchful,
    preparing myself more thoroughly
    day by day
    to meet you, my Lord,
    face to face.

Lord Christ,
    full of mercy and compassion,
    accept these prayers for your name's sake.

## *God meets our needs*

151    I bring all my concerns to you, heavenly Father,
        knowing you are always ready to listen
        and eager to help.

        I pray for your church,
            especially in its work of counselling
            and welcoming those in great need or difficulty;
            that our Christian witness
            may vividly reflect
            the generous love of Christ.

        I pray for the world's leaders
            and all in positions of authority and responsibility;
            that the world's resources may be justly shared
            so that all its inhabitants
            have enough for their needs.

        I pray for all refugees and asylum seekers,
            and those whose mental capacity
            makes them vulnerable to inadequate provision
            of food, clothing or housing.

        Loving God, make me more prepared
            to give my time, energy, talents and money
            in serving those in need
            and working hand in hand with Christ.

        Father of mercy,
            in thankfulness I welcome
            your Spirit into my life,
            and ask you to accept my prayers,
            through Jesus Christ, your Son.

## *The Light of God's glory*

Loving God, your glory is all around me.  *152*
I pray with a thankful and adoring heart.

I bring to you all those involved
  with teaching the Christian faith;
  our schools and Sunday schools,
  and missionaries – especially . . .
  *[any missionary project of special interest]*

I bring to you, Lord,
  all peoples of our earth
  with their different cultures,
  philosophies and traditions;
  multiracial communities,
  especially those experiencing problems
  with mutual understanding and harmony.

I bring to you all new-born babies,
  especially those who are unwanted
  or abandoned;
  all people who are elderly
  and approaching death,
  especially those who are frightened.

I bring to you my own local church,
  our programme for education and outreach,
  its areas of stagnation
  and its potential for growth.

Heavenly Father,
  accept these prayers,
  through Christ my Saviour.

99

## *Chosen and called*

153    Loving God,
         you have adopted me as your child;
         I pray to you now in the Spirit of Jesus Christ
         for all who are called to spread the news
         of hope and joy for humanity;
         that their teaching may be inspired
         so as to draw many to you, through Christ.

         I remember all decision makers and policy planners,
            that as they are guided by your will,
            the world may be governed and ordered wisely.

         I hold before you all who work with the sick;
            those who are chronically ill,
            or suffering from a long-term disability;
            that even through intense pain
            there may be positive, spiritual growth,
            and a deeper awareness of your presence.

         I pray for those who are called
            to care for children,
            through fostering, adoption,
            or in residential homes;
            also for children separated from their families,
            for those waiting to be placed
            in loving homes,
            for a greater sharing of love
            and the growth of mutual trust.

         Almighty Father,
            hear these prayers,
            and make me alert to your response,
            through Jesus Christ my Lord.

## Christ reigns in glory

Loving Father, I come to you                           *154*
   trusting in Christ's victory
   over all evil.

Bless and encourage all who witness to Christ
   in spite of danger and persecutions;
   all who work to bring others to Christ,
   that they may bear much fruit.

Guide world leaders, diplomats and advisers;
   that your will for the world may be done.

I bring to you all those
   who have never received your Good News;
   all places where violence and terrorism
   make normal life impossible;
   that the Spirit of the Prince of Peace
   may filter through to increase
   love and understanding,
   respect and goodwill.

Grant, Lord, to me
   and those with whom I live and work,
   that in everything we do,
   and every minute we live,
   you may be glorified
   and your will accomplished.

Father,
   trusting in your great love for us,
   I bring you these prayers
   through Jesus Christ my Lord.

## *Redeemed by Christ's suffering*

155    In gratitude for Christ's saving death,
    I pray to you, my loving Father,
    for all who, in following Christ,
    have encountered suffering,
    danger or persecution;
    that they may be supported and sustained
    by the presence of the suffering Christ.

    Sustain with your love the innocent who suffer
    as a result of the world's mistakes,
    ineptitudes, misplaced priorities or greed;
    that love may breach the walls of prejudice
    and bring fresh life to the deserts of hopelessness.

    I remember the aimless and bewildered;
    those who grieve
    and those who try to repress their grief;
    all who are finding a burden
    desperately hard to bear.

    I offer to you, O God,
    my own friends and loved ones
    as well as myself;
    that we may trust Jesus
    to bring good out of every situation,
    however hopeless it seems.

    Father, accept these prayers,
    through Jesus Christ.

# God with Us

## *Jesus, King of Love*

Christ, King of Love,                          *156*
    I come to you in prayer for all who are baptised,
    and especially those who have lost their faith
    or stopped praying;
    that they may be brought back
    through your love,
    and put into contact with those
    who can guide and reassure them.

Guide with your love all gatherings of people:
    all meetings, or political demonstrations,
    social and sporting events,
    that they offer enjoyment, and influence for good,
    rather than incite to violence and evil.

Let your love be known by those suffering
    from incurable or life-threatening diseases;
    those who are denied necessary medical care;
    and make me ready to use my time,
    money and influence,
    so that unnecessary suffering and death are avoided.

Remember, O Christ, my own loved ones,
    families and friends,
    and especially those from whom I am separated.

Be near to people who are missing from their homes
    and those who wait for them;
    let your powerful love
    be a protection against all evil.

O Christ, hear my prayer.

## *God comes to us with grace*

157    God my Father, I know you are always with me.
Grant that I,
    and all your Church,
    may be a sign of your presence in the world
    and bring many to the joy of living in your love.
I pray that in the world
    no evil may thwart your will,
    but rather that your kingdom
    may be established
    and your will fulfilled.

Be especially present to all who suffer
    mentally, physically and spiritually;
    and equally to those who see no further
    than immediate physical comforts,
    and do not realise their spiritual poverty.

May your presence be known in this community,
    to all who live and work within it;
    that we may strive each day
    to align ourselves
    with the life of Christ,
    who saves us from our sin.

Father,
    trusting in your mercy,
    I lay these prayers before you
    through Jesus Christ my Lord.

## Glorify God

Loving Father, my hope and my joy,         *158*
   come to me now, and to your whole creation.
   I pray for all those Christians
   who are persecuted for their faith;
   that they may be strengthened
   by the assurance of Christ's presence
   for all time and in all places.

I bring to your love all politicians
   and government ministers;
   that they may discern Christ's truth
   and be given the courage
   to walk faithfully in it.

Let me see you, loving Lord,
   in the malnourished and the starving,
   all who have become diseased
   from contaminated water supplies;
   that as fellow human beings
   we may be led by the love of Christ
   to share the world's resources.

Work your healing in this community,
   and especially the many groups
   of Christian people;
   may Jesus' love and desire for our unity
   inspire us to break down barriers
   and build bridges
   to your greater glory.

## Sharing the Good News

159    Lord Christ, as you approach me
        with welcoming arms,
        so I approach you and pray
        in your Spirit of humility and love.

    I bring to you the worried,
        the confused and the anxious;
        that in trusting you
        and laying their troubles before you
        they may experience the release
        and freedom
        that your love provides.

    Please use me and all Christians,
        from the very young to the very old,
        in witnessing to the reality
        of your presence
        by the lives we lead.
    Enable us to live more closely with you,
        so that we may see you more clearly,
        become more like you,
        and witness more effectively
        to your love.

## The Lord is my light

O heavenly Father,                                          *160*
  you guide me faithfully
  and enlighten my life.
I pray now that you will make me ready,
  as part of your church,
  to follow Christ wherever he leads,
  even if the direction is unexpected
  or demanding.

Give us such brightness of love
  that Christ may be revealed,
  turning the doubtful to faith,
  the despairing to hope,
  and the revengeful to forgiveness.
Bring all nations to rejoice
  in the light of goodness
  and reject the darkness of evil.

In my daily life,
  may no opportunity be lost
  for sharing the joy and peace of Christ
  with those I meet.

Father,
  I commend my whole life
  to your loving care,
  through Jesus Christ my Lord.

## The Family of God

161    Holy God, give me grace
to open the door of my home
to welcome Jesus;
may all Christian families
be an example and a source of strength,
in a ministry of warmth and generosity,
and the wider society be based
on mutual respect and understanding,
on co-operation and care.

I pray for all families who are suffering
through poverty, sickness,
separation or war;
that your presence
may comfort and strengthen them,
and that those around them may work in Christ
to ease their burdens
and minister to their needs.

I pray for my own family and loved ones,
both living and departed,
both those I feel close to
and those I find difficult
to understand,
and I name before you
those who are in particular need.

Father,
I ask you to hear my prayers,
through Jesus Christ my Lord.

## Jesus is here

Loving God, I turn,         *162*
   with my heart filled with thanksgiving
   towards you who loves me so completely,
   and pray that the joy
   and wonder of Christ's presence
   may infuse the lives of all your people,
   so that the Good News may be spread
   throughout the world.
May all families be blessed
   with his everlasting joy,
   and all homes filled
   with his peace.

I pray that all in authority
   may be filled with your wisdom
   and compassion
   and that the lonely,
   the rejected and the isolated
   may have knowledge and confirmation
   of your abiding warmth and love.

Father, accept my prayer:
   in wonder and adoration
   I offer my life to you,
   with and through
   the Lord Jesus Christ.

## *Waiting expectantly*

163    Loving God, since you have promised
     that Christ will return,
     I pray in hope and expectation
     for all Christian people;
     for increased love and commitment,
     to work within the world
     as yeast within the dough.

    I pray for those in authority,
     that they may base their priorities
     and decisions
     on the foundations of your power:
     justice and mercy.

    May those who suffer pain, grief or distress
     know your strength and support
     so that their very suffering
     may become a channel
     for your redeeming love.

    I pray for my own community,
     that your presence may be known
     in the varied, separate lives surrounding me;
     that, alerted to their needs,
     I may work in Christ,
     with all your church,
     to care and provide.

    Father, you came in Jesus
     to show the true way to life.
    Help me to progress along that way
     in your strength,
     through the same Jesus Christ my Lord.

## *Jesus is the Word made flesh*

God my Father,                                                    *164*
    you love me so dearly:
    I pray that the Word who became flesh
    may be so manifest in my life,
    and the lives of all Christians,
    that other people notice
    and are attracted to Jesus
    by the way we live and love;
    that the world may stop
    its noise, chatter and arguing
    long enough to recognise
    the Word of hope and peace.

Bless and support
    all expectant mothers
    and those in labour;
    that all new-born babies
    and young children
    may be cherished, loved
    and protected
    as they bear your love
    to the world anew.

May there be more
    understanding and mercy
    in our family relationships,
    with Christ always among us –
    not an occasional visitor.

Please hear my prayers which I offer
    through Jesus, your Son.

## *Guidance and correction*

165    Lord God, may your love
        spill out through your church
        to the world,
        filling all teaching,
        all advice and counsel,
        all correction and guidance.

May your Spirit
    of forgiveness and acceptance
    permeate the social and political
    fabric of the world
    until we are able to criticise gently,
    and accept criticism honestly;
    discuss differences calmly,
    and be prepared to negotiate rationally.

May your comfort and consolation
    soothe those who are afraid
    or in great pain,
    refresh those who are mentally
    or physically exhausted
    and be a lifeline to those
    who are brokenhearted or in despair.

May the light of Christ
    shine in all people's hearts
    to show us our faults
    and enable us to admit them;
    shine through our lives in
    the way we treat each other,
    especially when we disagree or feel hurt.
All this I pray
    through the merits of Jesus, my Saviour.

## Do not be afraid

Heavenly Father, I come to you full of wonder          *166*
   over your involvement with your creation,
   and asking your help for the world
   in all its injustice, cruelty and oppression;
   its confused priorities and lost opportunities,
   that all may be guided unceasingly
   by the compassionate leadership
   of your Spirit.

I pray for all who labour to spread the Good News,
   especially those who face threatening behaviour,
   imprisonment or persecution;
   for those who are tempted to remain silent
   in order to avoid danger;
   that they may trust in Christ's promise
   to keep them eternally safe.

I pray for all who are wounded, injured and in pain;
   that they may find Christ sharing in their suffering;
   and for all those who inflict pain on others,
   and all who are fired with hatred;
   that their lives may be transformed
   by encountering Christ, who loves them.

Bless my family, friends and neighbours;
   the very young and the very old;
   give us all wisdom to see opportunities
   of showing Christ's love,
   and enough energy and time
   to do what you need us to.

Merciful Father, hear these prayers
   for the sake of Jesus Christ.

## *Unity in diversity*

167    God the Three in One,
           hear my prayers for all situations of conflict:
       for the work of the church,
           especially where there is violent opposition,
           complacency or apathy,
           that people of all traditions and outlooks
           who work with Christ
           may be blessed and encouraged by your love.

       Look upon this world,
           with its mistakes and misunderstandings,
           all the breakdown in communication
           between individuals, groups or nations,
           that your unifying love
           may draw people together,
           to find common ground where they can build,
           rather than dwell on hurtful divisions.

       I pray for those without homes
           or living in crowded, inadequate accommodation;
           those living alone and isolated;
           for the hungry and malnourished;
           that your love, working through us, your body,
           may bring hope to those in desperate need.

       I pray for a greater love and fellowship
           in the Church, the community and in families;
           that your life living in us
           may make us more ready to listen,
           to respond and to forgive,
           to put ourselves out and seek to understand.
       Holy Trinity of love,
           hear my prayer.

## Christ, always present

In the knowledge of Christ's        *168*
   constant presence,
   I pray to you, heavenly Father,
   God of mercy and love,
   for the world-wide
   Christian community,
   that unceasing prayer and praise
   may be offered as our planet turns
   through night and day,
   that we may be strengthened and encouraged
   to reveal Christ to the world.

Give direction and guidance to the world;
   that in all areas of discussion, negotiation,
   policy-making and reform,
   Christ may be present,
   touching our lives and wills
   with his peace.

Comfort all those whose happiness
   is less because of war, homelessness,
   pain or separation from loved ones;
   that in all their troubles they may know
   through the humility of Christ's birth,
   life and death on this earth
   your immense love for us
   and your desire to share our suffering.

I pray for my home and family,
   that we may recognise Christ's presence,
   living among us,
   deepening and extending our love one for another.
   In his name, I pray.

## *Christ, our ever-present hope*

169   Loving God,
         trusting your constant faithfulness,
         I bring you my cares and concerns
         for all who are imprisoned or persecuted
         because of their faith;
         for the lapsed and the doubting;
         that they may know
         your sovereign presence in Christ,
         in all areas of life.

      In the world of commerce,
         trade and the media;
         may Christ's peaceful presence
         at the heart of busyness
         create channels for enlightenment and discernment.

      I pray for the malnourished,
         those whose land no longer supports them.
      Inspire us all to care for one another,
         to share the world's resources
         in mutual trust,
         and be living signs of hope
         to one another.

      Bless my family,
         that our day-to-day concerns
         may not blind us to your love,
         but rather be infused by it
         so that you are central in our lives,
         for the sake of Jesus, our Saviour.

# New Life in Christ

*Christ, the Resurrection and the Life*

In the presence of the risen Christ, 170
    I lift my heart to you, God the giver of all life.

I pray for all who are called
    to particular Christian ministries:
    all ordained ministers,
    theological students and teachers,
    that as they learn together
    they may grow in wisdom and humility
    and be increasingly filled
    with the life of Christ.

Transform with new life all bureaucracies
    which frustrate and delay
    the course of useful action;
    all areas of instability and political corruption;
    that whatever is good may flourish and grow,
    so that evil may be overcome
    and rendered powerless.
Strengthen all who suffer from pain or disease,
    and those who tend them.

Bless all who are engaged or newly married;
    for those coping with family problems,
    difficult circumstances or bereavement;
    that they may lean on the loving presence of Christ
    who dispels all fear and brings life and peace.

Thank you, Lord, for your constant
    life-renewing love.
Accept these prayers
    for the sake of your Son, Jesus Christ.

## *God, the giver of life*

171   Loving Father, from whom all life comes,
        I bring to your love all those
        who have committed their lives to Christ
        in ordained ministries;
        that they may grow into spiritual maturity,
        as freed sons and daughters of you.

     I bring to your love the world with its problems,
        mistakes and errors of judgement;
        that in every society
        your light may shine
        and your life and peace be known.

     Remember, O God, the deaf,
        the blind and the partially sighted,
        all those who are chronically ill
        and all who tend them;
        that even in all their hardships
        they may know life in all its fullness.

     I bring to your love all parents,
        all adoptive and foster parents,
        women labouring to bring new life
        into the world,
        that they may be blessed and strengthened
        by you who are life itself.

     Father, hear these prayers
        through Jesus Christ,
        in whom is life in abundance.

## *Word of eternal life*

Merciful Father, I bring to your love                    *172*
   all religious communities and organisations,
   who offer a constant wave of prayer
   as the earth spins;
   all who sense your call
   to a life of renewal
   and deeper commitment,
   that your will may be made clear to them.

I bring to your love all who wield power
   in each community of our world;
   those who persist in challenging
   injustice and prejudice;
   all who bring to public attention
   areas of need and unnoticed hardship
   where life is stifled or denied.

I bring to your love all those in hospital,
   in wards and on operating tables
   throughout the world;
   those worn down by constant pain;
   those who are struggling
   to rebuild broken lives.

I bring to your love
   all my hopes, doubts and fear;
   my responsibilities and difficulties
   at work and at home,

Heavenly Father,
   I offer you these prayers
   through Jesus Christ.

## *Celebrating resurrection*

173    In the hope and joy of resurrection,
        I pray to you, O God,
        for all who have been called by Christ
        to serve the world as his followers;
        that initial enthusiasm may not die
        but deepen to set us all on fire
        with his love.

I pray for a fairer distribution
        of the world's resources,
        so that life and hope are brought
        to the starving and homeless;
        for places where fear and violence rule;
        that peace and justice may be restored.

I pray for those who feel they are wasting their lives;
        for those under pressure
        at home or at work;
        for all who feel lost,
        uncertain or worthless;
        that your living power
        may stabilise, heal and recreate them.

I pray for myself, my friends and relatives,
        that in whatever troubles beset us
        we may open ourselves
        to the healing and renewing
        life of Christ,
        which has power to bring hope.
In his name, I pray.

## *Openness and humility*

Loving Father, I come before you        *174*
   with humility and love,
   open to your transforming grace,
   that you will bless me and all Christians
   striving to follow the Lord of Life;
   that we may not fall into the temptation
   of complacency or self-righteousness;
   that we may joyfully become the least important
   for Christ's sake.

I pray for all who are involved
   in the worldly struggles for power,
   all areas of political unrest,
   all decision- and policy-makers;
   that wisdom, common sense and respect
   may encourage just and peaceful government.

Remember the physically blind
   and their families;
   those who are spiritually blind
   and think they can see;
   those whose minds are confused
   through accidents, illness or age,
   may your inner sight
   bring enlightenment, order and peace.

Grant that I and all Christians
   may be increasingly open
   to the searing light of Christ,
   until our darkest corners are lit by his love.
Lord God, accept these prayers,
   through Jesus Christ.

## Good stewardship

175    Lord Christ, as I have committed myself to you,
        I pray in your Spirit
        that all Christians may witness
        to the value of caring,
        regardless of race or colour;
        that they may be maintained
        in your strength and humility,
        to serve the world in love.

Give grace to all monarchs, presidents,
        and those in powerful positions;
        those whom they govern,
        and those with whom they negotiate;
        that their great resources of power and wealth
        may be used for peace and justice
        over all our earth.

Remember the very poor,
        the weak and oppressed,
        the abandoned, rejected and abused;
        that all obstacles to their healing and wholeness
        may be removed by your presence,
        all blindness, prejudice and greed
        transformed into an outpouring of love and hope.

Lord, help me to see my own faults more clearly,
        acknowledge my weaknesses
        as well as my strengths,
        and offer both to you
        who can make me new.

## God's Spirit in us

Loving God, hear my prayers                    *176*
    for all those who form the church,
    in its variety and richness
    throughout the world;
    that we may be encouraged
    and strengthened
    and our weariness
    constantly refreshed
    by the living Spirit of Jesus.

Give grace to all councils, committees
    and governing bodies,
    to those serving on juries,
    to air, sea and mountain rescue teams,
    that in working together
    and enabled by your Spirit
    they may strive for what is good,
    just and honest.

I pray for the poor and for the hungry,
    for the blind, the downtrodden
    and those imprisoned;
    that your Spirit, alive in your people,
    will work your healing love.

For myself, I ask deeper insight,
    more awareness and greater love,
    so that I can more effectively
    serve the world
    as a living member of the body of Christ.

Father, hear my prayers,
    through Jesus Christ my Lord.

## *The life of the Spirit*

177    Almighty and everlasting God,
        I pray for your church,
        that in constant prayerfulness
        all Christians may be attentive
        and receptive to your life-giving Holy Spirit.

      In the world, with all its mistakes and tragedies,
        may your Spirit bring order,
        serenity and hope.

      May your generous Spirit of love
        bring light to the hearts.
        of all those whose lives
        are darkened by guilt,
        resentment and despair;
        those who live violent and cruel lives;
        for drug dealers
        and all who corrupt young minds;

      I pray for my loved ones
        and for those I find difficult to love;
        that your Spirit living in us
        will increase our love for each other.

      Father, accept these prayers,
        through Jesus Christ my Lord.

## *Love one another*

Loving heavenly Father,                          *178*
   thank you for sending Jesus
   to bring life and hope
   to the world.
Bless the work of the church
   in spreading his Good News,
   that the life of the whole world
   may be renewed by your love.

I pray for all those with authority
   and responsibility
   in governing the nations
   of this world:
   for peace, for compassion,
   forgiveness and generosity.

Be especially close to those who shut love out;
   those who have been hurt
   by lack of love;
   those whose love
   has become distorted
   and twisted into hate.

I pray for those among whom
   I live and worship;
   pour your love
   into our lives
   to transfigure, refresh
   renew and enrich,
   through Jesus Christ our Lord.

## *He who was dead is alive*

179    Loving God,
          I pray that Christ's risen life
          will infuse and activate
          all people and areas of creation:

          the church, especially missionaries
          both abroad and in this country,
          that with inner quietness
          they may be ready to listen
          to the voice of the Spirit;

          world leaders and their advisers,
          that nothing may tempt them from integrity,
          and that they may boldly work
          for what is good, honest and just;

          those who doubt,
          those who have lost their faith,
          and those whose faith is being tested,
          that they may know the assurance
          of your presence and your love;

          this local community,
          that we may serve Christ
          in caring for one another
          and encourage one another
          in the faith of our loving Lord.
     In his name I pray.

## Christ is risen!

Lord God, I pray               *180*
   that the world may be transformed
   by the light of Christ's resurrection:

   that the joy and conviction of Christians
   may be so radiant
   that all who are lost,
   weary and searching
   may be directed
   towards your lasting inner peace;

   that from every world crisis and tragedy
   some good may come;
   that every problem may become an opportunity
   for development and spiritual growth;

   that those in mental, physical
   or spiritual distress
   may recognise in their suffering
   the seeds from which hope may spring,
   looking towards the day when they share
   the joy and wholeness of all creation;

   that the newly born
   and indeed all children
   may be nurtured in caring families,
   and the elderly cherished
   in your wide accepting love;

   that I may be worthy
   of all your gifts and blessings.
Hear my prayer
   through Christ the risen Lord.

## *The hope of glory*

181    Loving, merciful Father,
        let your glory be known:

        in the church,
        that all Christians,
        guided and strengthened in hope,
        may be attentive to their calling;

        in the world,
        that all nations
        may be led to understand
        your way of love,
        and that all decisions
        may reflect your will;

        among the lonely and frightened,
        that they may experience your joy and peace,
        and the despairing may see
        in the resurrection
        the light of hope;

        in all our relationships,
        that we may proclaim the Good News
        of your saving love
        by the way we respond to one another;

        in the silence
        which you fill
        with love and hope.

Father, accept my prayer,
        through Jesus Christ.

## *Joy in commitment*

Loving heavenly Father,                    *182*
   through Jesus Christ,
   you have adopted me as your child.
Let your Spirit of God
   who anointed Jesus
   strengthen and uphold me
   and all Christians
   so that we flood the world
   with your saving love.

Help all those in positions of power
   to understand the fundamental need
   for your Spirit of truth,
   peace and compassion
   and commit themselves
   to your way of justice.

Enable any who are living under
   a burden of guilt
   to find repentance, freedom and joy
   in your forgiveness.

Fill your church with the life of Christ,
   that the quality and brightness
   of our lives
   may draw others into his love
   and peace.

In Jesus' name I pray.

## *Responding to God's call*

183    God, my Father,
        I commend to your love
        all who have been recently ordained;
        that the people may accept and love them
        and help them to grow in Christ.

      I commend to your wisdom
        all who wield power;
        that, recognising your call
        to justice and compassion,
        they may encourage reconciliation
        rather than revenge,
        friendship rather than aggression,
        and flexibility,
        rather than stubborn intransigence.

      I commend to your healing
        all who are ill or in pain,
        all who are recovering from surgery,
        all who depend on others
        for life and movement;
        any who long for friends
        who would visit them in their illness.

      I commend to your peace and joy
        my home and all the homes
        in this community,
        especially where there is conflict
        or distress;
        that, being dwelt in by Christ,
        our homes may speak to every visitor
        of his love.
      In Christ's name I pray.

## Come, Holy Spirit

Loving God, fill me anew                                    *184*
    with your Spirit of love
    as I pray for my Christian brothers and sisters
    and for the whole of your world.

May all who profess to be Christians
    allow the Spirit to penetrate their lives,
    prune them where necessary,
    realign, train and support them
    so that they produce good fruit.

May the same Spirit work
    through the common bond of humanity
    to draw people closer,
    develop international understanding
    and friendship,
    break down prejudice
    and generate peace.

May all who are damaged and scarred
    physically, mentally, emotionally or spiritually,
    be given wholeness and healing;
    and let all who are floundering and confused
    find assurance in Christ,
    the source of meaning,
    through his indwelling Spirit.

Help me to use well the gifts of the Spirit within me,
    walking cheerfully and thankfully
    in the way you have prepared for me,
    and delighting in every opportunity to serve,
    through Jesus Christ my Lord.

## Christ makes us whole

185   God of life and hope,
          hear my prayer for the work of the church
          in every country,
          especially where Christian witness
          brings danger;
          that the Spirit of Christ
          may nurture life and hope
          in the world's darkest areas.

      Offer new life to all who encourage others
          to squander their time, money or talents;
          all who lead others into drug addiction;
          that they may come to know Christ
          as the only treasure worth worshipping.

      Transform all whose characters
          have become hardened and twisted
          through jealousy, resentment or hatred;
          that they may at last recognise
          their need for repentance
          and come to Christ to be restored
          to the joy of new life in him.

      Thank you for all who help me
          to know Christ better,
          who turn me back to him
          when I wander away;
          that in humility I may always be glad to learn
          and ready to accept criticism,
          in order to grow as a Christian.
      In his name, I pray.

## Christ shows God's glory

In the power of the Holy Spirit,          *186*
   I pray to you, heavenly Father:

   for all newly baptised Christians,
   all preparing for baptism,
   and everyone involved
   in teaching the faith –
   that Christ's love may take root,
   grow, and produce good fruit
   to your glory;

   for the world's political leaders
   and all who influence them –
   that there may be mutual respect and courtesy,
   and a shared desire
   for peace and understanding;

   for those who carry heavy burdens
   of guilt or anxiety;
   for the very ill and the dying
   and for their loved ones
   who share their suffering –
   that the Spirit of Christ will comfort,
   soothe and strengthen them;

   for myself and my spiritual development;
   for all whom I irritate and annoy;
   for any I have unwittingly hurt or damaged –
   that in fixing my gaze on Jesus,
   I may see my true self more clearly,
   for the sake of Jesus Christ.

## *Repent: the kingdom is near*

187    Caring heavenly Father,
          I pray for the coming of your kingdom:

          that Christians throughout the world
          may wholeheartedly follow Christ,
          so that their lives witness to the beauty
          and peace of his kingdom;

          for all world leaders,
          governments and their advisers,
          that they may be inspired
          to lead their people wisely and fairly,
          with understanding and sensitivity;

          for all those who feel trapped
          by the emotional, financial
          or political circumstances
          of their lives,
          that in Christ they may find
          freedom and vitality;

          for my own family and loved ones,
          especially any from whom we are separated,
          that we may learn to see Christ in each face,
          and serve him in caring for each other.

      Father of all time and space,
          accept these prayers
          through Jesus Christ our Lord.

# Faith, Trust, Hope

## *Hope in Christ*

Heavenly Father, I pray in faith,       *188*
   trusting in your infinite mercy.

Bless all Christian people,
   especially those whose faith
   has been battered
   through disaster and suffering,
   that they may know
   the assurance of your abiding presence
   which transforms and rebuilds.

Guide all administrative bodies
   and political institutions;
   that they may be always aware
   of the real needs of those they serve,
   and be effective
   in providing for them.

Comfort the dying
   and those who love and tend them;
   console the bereaved and desolate,
   that they may draw strength
   from the reality of Christ's life
   and his victory over death.

Enliven this local community
   with all its needs and cares,
   that we may be ready to serve Christ
   and spread his life-giving hope and joy.

God my Father, hear my prayer,
   and help me to do your will,
   through Jesus Christ.

## Faithfulness

189   Ever-present God,
        I pray to you in faith:

            for the church,
            that all Christian leaders
            may be given insight and understanding
            to guide their people
            into the light of God's truth;

            for all councils, committees
            and conferences,
            that a spirit of integrity
            may underlie all discussion
            and a desire for goodness
            inspire all decisions;

            for those in pain or distress,
            physically, emotionally
            or spiritually,
            that they may hold to you
            through all the bad times,
            trusting in your love
            which never fails;

            for all families,
            especially those who have troubles,
            that they may not be damaged
            through their suffering,
            but rather grow
            in compassion and understanding.

        Father, I ask all this
            through Jesus Christ my Lord.

## *God awaits our response*

God my Father, you love me;                    *190*
   help me to respond in faith
   and in prayer.

Nurture a deeper trustfulness
   among all Christian people,
   so that they may become
   more and more open
   to your will.

Let Love make her home
   in the hearts of people
   all over the world,
   to guide, sustain
   and renew.

Fill every family
   with the life of Christ,
   to know his joy
   and his transforming love.

Bless all expectant mothers,
   and the children growing within them,
   the babies being born today,
   and those children
   who are neglected or abused.

In thankfulness I ask you, Father,
   to hear my prayers,
   through Christ my Lord.

## *Loving and trusting God*

191    Creator God, I pray trustingly
        to you who make and sustain all people:

        for all who profess themselves Christians,
        that in fastening our eyes on Christ
        we may be led to unity;

        for the political, industrial
        and commercial administrations
        throughout our planet,
        that our material and economic organisation
        may reveal good stewardship
        of the gifts you have provided;

        for all convicted prisoners,
        and for the victims of their crimes;
        for all who are eaten up
        with hatred or jealousy;
        for all who are finding it impossible
        to forgive their enemies;

        for the homes and families around me;
        for loved ones who are separated
        by distance or death;
        for a deepening love towards each other
        in all our relationships.

Father,
        with grateful thanks for the gift of life,
        I offer you these prayers
        together with myself
        for your service;
        in Jesus' name I pray.

## *Wholeness and harmony*

Loving heavenly Father,                    *192*
   I ask that your love, peace and joy
   may fill all creation:

   the church in every corner of the earth,
   that your name may be held holy
   in unending waves of praise;

   all negotiators and administrators,
   guiding them to work with sensitivity,
   care and integrity;

   all marriages, especially those under strain,
   that those whose lives
   have been damaged or warped
   may be emotionally repaired
   and rebuilt;

   all our homes,
   so that when storms come
   they may stand firm
   on the solid rock of Christ.

Father of compassion and mercy,
   accept these prayers,
   through the person of Jesus Christ.

## *Struggling with faith*

193    I pray with confidence and faith
to the true and living God:

for the newly baptised
and the recently ordained;
for those who have rejected
their former faith,
and those who are besieged by doubt;

for those under pressure,
who are tempted
to compromise your values
of truth and love;
for all who make
far-reaching decisions;

for all the victims of power struggles,
suffering poverty, neglect,
disease and malnutrition;
for all whose health has been wrecked
by insanitary living and working conditions;

for myself,
for my neighbours and our friends,
for any I have hurt or offended;
for any who have hurt or offended me.

Most loving and merciful Father,
I ask you to take over my life
and live through it,
and accept these our prayers
in the name of Jesus.

## *Let the seeds grow*

Father, you have rooted and grounded me in Christ. *194*
I call to mind now, in prayer, all those in need.

I pray that all who teach the Christian faith
　　may be given appropriate language
　　to get through to those who hear,
　　so that your word takes root
　　in many hearts.

I pray that all diplomats and negotiators
　　may promote peace and friendship
　　between the nations,
　　fostering mutual respect
　　and understanding.

I pray that those whose lifestyle
　　has been threatened or shattered
　　by crippling illness or injury
　　may find within their suffering
　　the seeds of hope,
　　bringing new meaning to their lives
　　and transforming their outlook.

I pray that I and my family, neighbours and friends
　　may become daily more Christlike
　　and less self-centred;
　　more responsive to the needs of those around us,
　　and less bothered by what we as individuals
　　get out of life.

Father, hear my prayer
　　through Jesus Christ my Lord.

## *Trust in Jesus*

195    In the Spirit of Jesus
    I pray to you, heavenly Father.

I bring to your love
    all those who are being trained
    for ministry in the church;
    that their studies may teach them
    not only knowledge but perception,
    not only skills but sensitivity.

I bring to your love
    all whose positions of responsibility
    cause pressure and stress;
    that in their weakness and weariness
    they may come to Christ for refreshment,
    and rely upon him for their strength.

I bring to your love all who are dying;
    that their trust in Jesus may deepen,
    until their fears are calmed
    and they can look forward with real hope
    to meeting their Saviour face to face.

I bring to your love
    my own friends and loved ones;
    all who live with me and near me;
    all who rely on me,
    and all who are influenced
    by my behaviour.

God of all mercy, my hope and my joy,
    hear my prayers, for Jesus' sake.

## *Out of death, life*

Loving Father, I come to you                    *196*
   filled with the hope and joy
   of resurrection faith.

I pray for the newly baptised
   and their families;
   for those who are sensing your call
   and need reassurance in it;
   for all your people
   in every part of the world.

I pray for the areas in which there is fighting,
   unrest and unresolved conflict;
   for the unprincipled, the corrupt
   and those who thirst for revenge.

I pray for those who are finding life difficult
   at the moment;
   for those who are coping
   with personal tragedy or mourning;
   for all who are ill or frail.

I pray for neighbours here; in this street;
   and at school and at work;
   for any who may be wishing
   they knew someone
   willing to share their burden.

Father, in the name of the risen Jesus,
   I ask you to bring the hope,
   healing and joy of the resurrection
   to all these people for whom I pray.

## *Love beyond price*

197    Heavenly Father, I pray to you,
        trusting in your deep love,
        for the grace and strength
        to be obedient, as Christ was,
        in whatever you ask me to do,
        without thought
        for personal gain or safety.

    I pray for greater trust and friendship
        between the different nations
        on our planet;
        for a universal desire for peace,
        and the willingness to take
        the risks it demands.

    I pray for Christ's calming reassurance
        to bring peace of mind and spirit
        to those worried about the future,
        those dreading some difficult event,
        and those who are frightened of dying.

    I pray for the capacity to be positive
        and encouraging
        in all my relationships;
        for the right words to say
        in order to be a peacemaker
        and witness to your
        immeasurable love.

    Father, with a thankful heart
        I offer these concerns
        though Jesus Christ, my Saviour.

## The risk of faith

Loving heavenly Father,                          *198*
   I pray in confidence to you
   because you know me so well.

Into your enlightenment
   and perception
   I bring all whose faith is limited
   by fear or prejudice;
   all whose living faith
   has been replaced
   by the empty shell of habit.

Into the depths of your wisdom
   and understanding
   I bring those with responsibilities,
   and all who have difficult decisions to make;
   all those in charge of hospitals,
   schools, factories and community services.

Into the gentleness of your healing love
   I bring all who are in pain;
   all those recovering from surgery;
   those involved in crippling accidents
   or suffering from wasting diseases.

Into your tireless faithfulness
   I bring any who rely on me
   for help, support, guidance or encouragement;
   any whom I am being asked to serve
   or introduce to your love.

Father hear my prayers
   through your Son, Jesus Christ.

## *Let faith be real*

199　Heavenly Father, I draw near to you
　　　　with my needs and cares,
　　　　asking for your help and blessing.

　　　Bless and encourage all those who serve you;
　　　　inspire their teaching,
　　　　nudge their memories,
　　　　instruct them through their failure
　　　　and mature them through their experiences,
　　　　so that in all their undertakings,
　　　　your will may be done.

　　　Direct and guide the people of the world
　　　　towards harmony and peace,
　　　　mutual respect and appreciation
　　　　of one another's cultures and traditions,
　　　　so that we are prepared to learn from each other.

　　　Ease the burdens of those who are bowed down
　　　　with grief, depression, pain or guilt;
　　　　encourage the timid and frightened;
　　　　refresh all who are overworked
　　　　or have been unable to sleep,
　　　　and break down all barricades
　　　　of hatred and revenge.

　　　I ask you into my home and workplace;
　　　　may all friendships and business transactions,
　　　　shopping and leisure time,
　　　　be opportunities for rejoicing in your love
　　　　and spreading your peace.

　　　Father, in your love accept my prayers,
　　　　in Jesus' name.

## God saves and sends us

Heavenly Father, I pray trustingly,        *200*
   knowing that you care for us all:

   for those involved in missionary work
   all over the world,
   that their work may be blessed and fruitful,
   and that they may be constantly
   strengthened and encouraged
   by the caring presence of Christ;

   for the leaders and advisers of all nations;
   for diplomats, envoys and negotiators
   in all areas of difficulty,
   where tact and delicacy are needed;
   that people may learn to respect
   and honour one another;

   for all who are harassed and dejected,
   overworked, stressed or bewildered,
   that they may come to know
   the liberating calm of your peace
   beneath all the activity and clamour;

   for increased trust and faithfulness
   in my own life;
   for clearer knowledge of your will
   in how my time and ability is used;
   for a greater readiness
   to listen to your voice
   and respond to your calling.

Father, hear these prayers
   through Jesus Christ my Saviour and brother.

## *The assurance of things not seen*

201    Loving God, I pray to you now
        for the deepening of faith
        among all Christians;
        that our whole lives may rest
        in the joy and security of knowing
        that you are alive and in charge.

    I pray for the spreading of the Good News
        throughout the world,
        so that whatever important decisions are made
        and policies planned,
        people may work
        in harmony with you, their creator,
        for goodness, peace and reconciliation.

    I pray for the healing
        and repairing of broken lives,
        for vision and enlightenment
        among those darkened by fear and hatred;
        that your living Spirit, let loose,
        may anoint and soothe,
        pacify and recharge.

    I pray for a more loving atmosphere
        in my home, church and this community;
        more care and concern for each other,
        more willingness to forgive,
        understand and respect
        those with whom we live.

    Father, I ask you to accept these prayers,
        for the sake of Jesus Christ.

## *God confronts the world in Christ*

Father, knowing that you love me,  202
    I come to you with my prayers.

I  pray for more courage among all Christians;
    that we may stand up against evil and injustice,
    wherever we find it,
    trusting in your power
    and without thought for personal safety.

I pray for those countries at war;
    where there is distrust and suspicion;
    that peace may never be dismissed
    as an impossible dream,
    but acknowledged
    as the only real victory.

I pray for those who are living
    through a personal crisis at the moment;
    those who do not know which way
    to turn for the best;
    that your will may be made clear to them,
    so that they are guided and comforted.

I pray for my own life and family,
    that we may all know what work
    you are calling us to do,
    and trust you enough to obey your will.

Father,
    your glory fills and confronts the world,
    and so I entrust my cares to you.
    in the name of Jesus.

## Christ has overcome evil

203  As a follower of the way of Christ,
     I bring to you, Lord, the needs of this time.

I pray for your blessing
     on all who confess belief in you;
     that they may witness powerfully
     to your unselfish love and humility
     by the way they act and the lives they lead.

I pray for your blessing
     on all who administer justice,
     those working in law courts or serving on juries,
     and those who make laws,
     that they may be given insight and integrity.

I pray for your blessing
     on all those in prison or on probation;
     all those living in acute poverty;
     on all who are working among them
     to heal, redirect, support and encourage.

I pray for your blessing on me
     as I examine my life
     and draw closer to you;
     that through self-discipline and prayer
     I may enter your stillness,
     and know your will for me.

Father, accept these prayers,
     through Jesus Christ my Lord.

## Grace and strength come from God

Loving heavenly Father,                                    204
   I bring you my needs and cares.

I pray for deepening of prayerfulness
   among all Christians,
   that firmer faith and greater openness
   will lead to a rediscovery
   of your love and purpose.

I pray for the world,
   especially for areas of degradation
   and moral decay;
   that there may be a turning away
   from self-indulgence to self-discipline;
   from deception to integrity;
   from lawlessness to ordered peace.

I pray for those damaged or injured
   by violent abuse or terrorism;
   for all victims of war and rebellion,
   and for those who are responsible.

I pray for your strength
   in my own life,
   especially in those areas
   I know to be weak and open to temptation;
   that I may rely more and more on your power
   so that I live in you and you in me.

Father, hear these prayers,
   for the sake of Jesus Christ.

## *Wholeness and unity*

205   Heavenly Father, in humility,
      I bring to your love my cares.

I bring to you
   the divided Christian community;
   that you may bring about wholeness and unity.

I bring to you
   the divided world,
   split between wealth and poverty,
   complacency and oppression;
   that you may break through barriers
   with the power of love
   and reconciliation.

I bring to you
   all who are disfigured by disease,
   disadvantaged mentally or physically,
   and all whom society prefers to ignore;
   that your love may nourish and heal,
   restore and accept.

I bring to you
   the wounds and hurts of my own life
   and my family;
   all unresolved tensions and sorrows,
   all reunions, joys and healing;
   that you will bless our lives with your presence.

Heavenly Father,
   to whom all glory belongs,
   accept these prayers,
   through Christ my Lord.

## Complete forgiveness

Merciful Father, I pray in humility:                    *206*

> for the church, the body of Christ;
> for each one of its members who has lapsed
> or drifted away;
> for those who are struggling
> against doubt and temptation;
>
> for the many peoples of this earth;
> for the spread of justice,
> respect and goodwill;
> for a greater capacity to forgive
> and restore,
> and a weakening
> of hardened revenge;
>
> for those who suffer through neglect,
> famine, natural disasters or war;
> also for those who,
> through their own fault,
> now suffer;
>
> for myself and others;
> for those I find difficult
> to get on with,
> those I envy, admire or despise,
> that my love may be open and generous,
> wide and strong.

Merciful Father,
> accept these prayers,
> in the name of your Son Jesus Christ.

## *Welcoming Christ*

207   Heavenly Father, I lay before you:

the misunderstandings,
mistakes and foolishness
in the members of Christ's body, the Church;
that through learning humility and forgiveness
even our weaknesses may become
a source of strength and renewal;

all worldly distrust, revenge and corruption,
all deceit and injustice;
that your loving Spirit may inspire,
guide, repair and renew,
even where the darkness is deepest;

all those whose busy lives
leave little time for stillness;
the overworked –
those suffering from stress and exhaustion;
that they may find your inner peace
and constant strength and refreshment;

all the relationships in my everyday life;
the ordering of my own timetable;
that living closely with Christ
I may learn how to make room
for the important things
of eternal significance.

God our Father, hear my prayer;
and help me fix my life on you,
through Jesus Christ my Lord.

## *Peace*

In the peace of my Creator and sustainer, I pray:     *208*

    for the church throughout the world,
    especially in areas of apathy,
    and rejection of spiritual values;
    that through Christian witness
    many may come to find peace
    and fulfilment
    in Jesus, the Saviour;

    for all places of conflict;
    for countries at war;
    for all areas of violence and bloodshed,
    bitterness and hatred;

    for all who are distressed, bewildered,
    lost or confused;
    for those making painful decisions;
    for those who have no one to turn to for help;
    that they may be given guidance,
    comfort and serenity;

    for myself,
    the special needs and concerns known to me,
    for my own spiritual growth;
    that my ordered life may proclaim
    the beauty of your peace.

Father, knowing that you alone
   have the words of eternal life,
   I lay my prayers before you,
   through Christ my Lord.

## *Living the faith*

209    God my Father, I bring before you
my needs and concerns.

I pray for the church,
its leaders and all the faithful;
that in setting our hearts steadfastly
on the eternal truth of your love,
we may be nourished and yield good fruit.

I pray for those working in the news media;
for all whose words influence human society;
that integrity and honour may be valued
and responsibility never abused.

I pray for those who delight in scandal and gossip,
and for those whose reputations
are damaged by others,
that your love will heal and renew,
challenge and convert.

I pray for my own church fellowship,
its worship, learning and social groups,
that our genuine love for one another,
and desire for one another's good,
may cleanse our hearts from all envy,
intolerance or spitefulness.

God my Father,
in my weakness may I rely
on your constant and almighty strength.
I ask you to hear my prayer,
through Jesus Christ my Lord.

## *Trust in God brings peace and joy*

Heavenly Father, in faith I bring to you          *210*
   my burdens and cares:

   all who teach the Christian faith
   by word and example;
   that Christ will work,
   even through their weakness,
   to reach the world;

   all who are striving
   for peace and harmony
   in local government,
   national and international negotiations;
   that nothing may deter or divert them,
   so that your will
   may be done on earth;

   all who trust in worldly solutions or systems,
   those whose ideals lead them
   not to peace but to violence;
   that they may see the great rewards
   which come from living and trusting
   in you, the God of selfless love;

   my own personal faith,
   and my lack of faith;
   my own efforts to reconcile,
   and my sorrow for where these have failed;
   I offer you myself,
   and ask you to increase my faith and trust.

I commend all my cares to you,
   through Jesus Christ my Lord.

## *Love is the greatest gift*

211   Heavenly Father, I pray to you,
        trusting not in myself but in your mercy.

      I pray for a constant renewal
        in the church;
        for a ceaseless deepening of love
        and thankfulness.

      I pray for the world in which I live;
        for more tolerance
        and forgiveness
        among its people;
        for more understanding
        and less fear;
        for more friendship
        and less bitterness.

      I pray for all who hate,
        for all who seek revenge,
        for all who refuse to forgive;
        that love may transform
        their hearts and minds.

      I pray for the people around me here;
        that, being open to your grace,
        our community may be more deeply filled
        with your Spirit of outgoing love.

      God my Father, hear these prayers;
        give us all those qualities of faith,
        hope and love which last for ever.
      In Jesus' name I pray.

## *Christ, the Good Shepherd*

Christ, the Good Shepherd,         *212*
    hear me as I pray for the needs
    of all my brothers and sisters.

Guide your church,
    in its various ministries
    that it may never lead any astray,
    but always follow faithfully where you lead.

Let your love guard the world,
    that in striving to do God's will
    we may not abuse or waste our talents
    in thoughtless destruction,
    but rather work with you
    to heal, conserve and fulfil.

Tend those who are ill,
    and those who look after them;
    that even in pain and discomfort
    they may recognise you,
    who also suffered,
    and are full of caring and compassion.

Help me and my family
    to hear and respond to your call;
    that in following you, the Shepherd,
    we may be liberated
    to live selfless, generous lives.

Lord Jesus, hear my prayer;
    in joy may I follow your way,
    for you alone have the words of eternal life.

## *God seeks the lost*

213    God our Father,
>you come to welcome your people
>while we are still far off.
>So I pray in confidence.

>Reassure all lapsed Christians,
>>all who have lost their faith;
>>that they may return to you
>>and find you ready to welcome them home.

>Keep me aware of people
>>who have been made redundant,
>>or whose work is unhealthy or dangerous;
>>that I may strive to uphold
>>each person's dignity
>>and ease each person's burden.

>Make me a friend to the rejected and the homeless,
>>those who have become bitter and twisted
>>or hard and mean;
>>that the generous warmth of your love
>>will work within them
>>to thaw what is frozen,
>>strengthen what is weak,
>>heal what is hurt and repair what is damaged.

>Bless my home,
>>that it may spread the Good News
>>of Christ's redeeming love
>>by the way it reflects his peace,
>>his understanding and his joy.
>In his name I pray.

## *Be reconciled to God*

Lord, may the good news of your salvation      *214*
   never be taken for granted
   but accepted and shared
   with thankfulness and joy.

Give all nations the courage
   to fight against what is evil
   and to nurture what is good
   in an atmosphere of respect
   and consideration for others.

Bless those whose lives
   have been twisted and spoilt by sin;
   that the lost and weary
   may turn to you the God of love
   for guidance and peace.

Remember all who live in this district;
   that we may use our gifts
   in serving one another
   and spreading the love of Jesus
   throughout the world.

Father, I ask all these things
   through Jesus Christ my Lord.

## *Jesus gives sight to the blind*

215    Lord Jesus, you gave sight to the blind.

I pray that wherever there is blindness,
   prejudice or lack of vision in the Church,
   you will work your healing power
   to refresh, enlighten and transform.

Wherever personality conflicts,
   errors of judgement or insensitivity
   threaten peace,
   may your Spirit enable us
   to work towards harmony and goodwill.

Come to all who are troubled and distressed
   by pain, illness, poverty, hunger
   or any other suffering,
   that they may experience
   your personal love, loyalty and healing.

Make me more sensitive
   to the needs of those with whom
   I live and work;
   less critical,
   and better prepared
   to encourage and forgive.

Lord Jesus,
   you pour out your blessings so richly on me;
   with thankful heart I praise you,
   and ask you to hear my prayers,
   for your name's sake.

## Overcome evil with good

Loving Father, hear my prayers:                    *216*

    for all lapsed Christians
    and all whose faith is being tested;
    all whose spiritual growth is being stunted
    by material cares or possessions;
    and all who are hesitantly approaching Jesus
    for the first time
    or after long separation from him;

    for the areas in which corruption
    has splintered the integrity of government;
    for the instances
    of double dealing and hypocrisy,
    which blunt honour
    and breed suspicion and revenge;

    for all who are trapped and frustrated
    by physical or mental disabilities,
    illness or weakness;
    for the lonely
    and those for whom no one prays.

    for enlightenment as to our own areas
    of spiritual weakness;
    for the courage to desire real,
    fundamental changes there,
    and for the will to persevere in growing.

Most merciful Father,
    accept my prayers
    in the name of Jesus.

## *God has power to forgive*

217    Knowing that your deep love surrounds me
      and reaches out to me in every distress,
      I unload my burdens of care to your healing power,
      heavenly Father.

I bring before you the Church's work
      among the homeless,
      the disillusioned and the apathetic,
      in communities all over the world.

I bring before you all areas of the world
      where lack of communication
      breeds suspicion and fear;
      where lack of understanding
      breeds insecurity and a spirit of revenge.

I bring before you all whose lives
      are crippled by unrepented sin
      or the refusal to forgive;
      all whose lives are constantly restless
      and devoid of peace.

I bring before you each member of this community,
      each anxiety and sorrow,
      each hope and dream,
      each weakness and special need.

Heavenly Father, so full of power
      and yet so personally involved,
      accept these prayers
      and let your will be done in the world,
      through Jesus Christ we pray.

## Return to God

Loving God, my creator and sustainer,    *218*
    hear my prayers for the Church and the world.

I bring to your love
    all who have committed their lives
    to your service;
    that they may all be one,
    bound together by your Holy Spirit.

I bring to your love
    all the areas of the world
    in which there is hostility and unrest;
    that new routes to negotiation
    and reconciliation may emerge.

I bring to your love
    all who have become hard and aggressive
    through years of festering hate or jealousy;
    that their unresolved conflicts
    may be brought to your light and healed.

I bring to your love
    the members of my own family,
    especially when we find it difficult
    to get together or understand;
    that our love for one another
    may enter a new dimension
    of warm and positive caring,
    seasoned with laughter.

Lord and Father, hear my prayers,
    through Jesus Christ my Saviour.

## *Love God and your neighbour*

219    Loving God, humbled by the wonder
of your love for creation,
I bring before you my concerns:

all Christians who are troubled by doubt,
all who have lapsed from worshipping
or whose prayer time is threatened by busyness;
that they may know the nearness of Christ,
and be touched by his calm and stillness.

the heated arguments, industrial disputes,
blinkered vision and stubbornness of our world;
that the power of your love may soften,
ease and coax us all
to be more understanding, wise and forgiving.

widows, widowers and orphans,
all broken families and the socially rejected;
those who are disfigured or incapacitated;
that the warmth of your love may radiate
all aspects of life, even the most painful,
to heal, comfort and transform.

the dark, shadowed areas of my own life;
that in the light of your love
I may see my weaknesses more clearly
and notice the needs around me more readily,
so that in Christ's strength
I can show love in practical ways

Father, work your love in my life,
and accept these prayers,
through Jesus Christ my Lord.

## God's infinite kindness

Confident in the love of Christ,                    *220*
   I bring my needs and cares to you, heavenly Father.

I pray for all lapsed Christians;
   all who have known Christ but rejected him;
   all who doubt his love or are hesitant
   to trust him with their lives;
   that they may all be led back
   to his welcoming arms.

I pray for this world
   with its weaknesses, self-indulgence and greed,
   its misplaced affections
   and well-meant interference;
   that lives may be ordered and calmed
   by the breath of Christ's Spirit.

I pray for all missing persons
   and their families;
   all who have lost their way emotionally
   or professionally;
   that all who are lost may be found,
   and know the security
   of being loved and protected
   by their creator.

I pray for my own life;
   that it may be reordered,
   calmed and refreshed by your Holy Spirit,
   and healed of all that shuts me off
   from your love.
   In Jesus' name I pray.

## *Christ renews and transforms*

221    Loving Father, I pray
        for the healing of divisions
        among all who follow Christ;
        that filled with hope by his resurrection
        we may be inspired to break down barriers
        to forgiveness and reconciliation.

        Give grace to all who hold positions
        of responsibility and leadership,
        both internationally
        and in our own community;
        that they themselves may be led by your Spirit
        to make wise decisions
        and help create a humane and caring world.

        Renew all who incite others to antisocial,
        addictive or criminal behaviour,
        that they may be transformed and redirected;
        strengthen the weak, lonely, young and depressed,
        who are so vulnerable to their temptations;
        that they may resist the pressures around them.

        Bless my family and all families;
        our hopes and sorrows,
        difficulties and celebrations;
        that all our relationships
        may be bathed in the love of Christ,
        full of tenderness and compassion.

        Father,
        I ask you to hear these prayers
        through Jesus Christ my Lord.

## *Christ gives new meaning to life*

Father God, I pray to you:                              *222*

    for all Christian leaders
    of all denominations;
    for the healing of old wounds,
    for forgiveness and an openness
    to the Holy Spirit
    who alone can make us one;

    for areas of poverty,
    overcrowding and neglect;
    of depression and high unemployment;
    that, working through your faithful people,
    you may bring to the world the freshness
    and vitality of hope and caring love;

    for all who are trapped
    by disability, illness or addiction;
    all who feel unwanted or rejected;
    that they may experience as a living reality
    the liberation of Christ's accepting love;

    for the areas of my own life
    which need to be remade in Christ;
    for any trying or difficult relationships,
    people I tend to criticise or despise;
    that your uncompromising love
    may inspire me to give without limits
    and without exceptions.

Father, accept these prayers
    through Jesus Christ,
    and use me for your glory.

## *Christ, the anointed King*

223     Lord God, in the name of Christ:

       I pray for the Church
          as it works to reconcile humanity;
          that Christians may speak
          in words the world understands,
          advising wisely, counselling lovingly
          and welcoming wholeheartedly.

       I pray for the needs of each community;
          that wherever feelings have boiled over
          and are out of control,
          the calm reassurance of Christ
          may restore harmony and goodwill.

       I pray for those attending hospitals and clinics,
          those in residential homes;
          for their relatives and friends,
          and the staff who look after them;
          that they may be sustained, strengthened,
          and brought to wholeness
          by your healing love.

       I pray for all who lead lonely, unhappy lives;
          all whose marriages are crumbling;
          all who cannot cope
          with the demands of family life;
          that you will give to those who can help
          perception and the courage to act.

       In Jesus' name I pray,
          and through him I offer myself
          to be used in your service.

# Worship, Discipleship, Mission

*God wants mercy, not sacrifice*

Heavenly Father,　　　　　　　　　　　　　　　*224*
   in thankfulness for your constant
   love and loyalty,
   I bring you my needs and concerns.

Inspire those involved in the planning
   and leading of your Church's worship;
   that it may be an outward expression
   of deep, personal commitment
   and never become careless
   or empty repetition.

Motivate those involved in welfare services,
   prison management,
   and those working in industry and commerce;
   all whose work helps maintain peace and order;
   that justice may always be administered with mercy,
   and policies grounded in loving care.

Challenge all who have become
   prisoners of habits,
   whether drugs, self-indulgence
   or constant criticism;
   help us break those habits in ourselves,
   enabling mutual support and encouragement
   as we recognise our mutual
   needs and weaknesses.

Father of mercy,
   I rejoice at your welcoming forgiveness,
   and ask you to accept my prayers
   through Jesus Christ our Lord.

## *Christ is our King*

225   Lord Christ, acknowledging your kingship,
     I ask your blessing
     on the church and on the world.

     I pray for the work
      of your body the Church,
      that all may labour zealously
      until the world is drenched
      in your peace, joy and love.

     Bless and equip with your love
      all peacemakers and reformers;
      all who work for justice,
      reconciliation and harmony.

     Encourage those who heal and tend
      the injured, sick and dying,
      and those in their care;
      all involved in medical research
      and those whose lives depend
      on drugs, dialysis or radiotherapy.

     Enable me to dedicate my energies
      and resources more fully
      to establishing your kingdom;
      that I may undertake every task
      and activity joyfully
      in the strength of my King.
     For your name's sake I pray.

## *Endurance and reward*

God my Father,                                                      *226*
    I lay at your feet my needs and cares,
    praying in the Spirit of Jesus.

I lay at your feet your Church:
    the need for ministry and leadership,
    for a firm witness by all Christians
    in the face of materialism and oppression.

I lay at your feet the needs
    of our divided, fractious world;
    its systems, schemes, fashions and disasters;
    that your kingdom of love
    may be established on earth,
    as it is in heaven.

I lay at your feet the needs of all who suffer
    in earthquakes, floods, droughts,
    famine and epidemics;
    all who try to supply relief and medical aid;
    that in Christ we may labour
    for the good of the world.

I lay at your feet
    the needs of this community;
    the local problems and injustices;
    the involvement of Christians
    in this corner of your world.

God my Father,
    trusting in your constant care and protection,
    I bring you these prayers
    in the name of Jesus.

## *Forgiven and forgiving*

227    Father God, you love me so dearly.
        I bring to you my concerns for your world.

        I pray for the spreading of the gospel
            throughout all countries and cultures;
            for all those working to reconcile people
            with you their creator;
            for all involved in counselling
            and spiritual teaching.

        I pray for a deepening spirit
            of fellowship and goodwill
            among the people of this earth;
            for a greater willingness to forgive,
            negotiate, communicate and support.

        I pray for all victims of aggression;
            for those obsessed with hatred and retaliation;
            for the injured, the abused and the dying.

        I pray for your guidance and restoration
            in my own life;
            for more awareness of my faults
            and areas of blindness;
            for a greater understanding
            of your love for me.

        Heavenly Father,
            trusting in your amazing love,
            I ask you to accept these prayers,
            through Jesus Christ our Lord.

## *Persevere in prayer*

Everlasting and unchanging Father,                     *228*
   quieten my heart, that I may pray.

I pray for all those involved
   in the ceaseless praying
   on our spinning earth;
   for all contemplative orders;
   for those rooted in prayer;
   and for those learning to pray
   or who feel they cannot pray.

I pray for the world,
   for victory of good over evil
   in situations of international
   or local significance;
   for a deepening of trust
   and a desire for truth and peace.

I pray for the disheartened and uninspired;
   for those whose lives are frustrating
   and endlessly stressful;
   for the homeless and unemployed;
   and for those addicted to drugs,
   alcohol or gambling.

I pray for my own family
   with their particular needs;
   for local shopkeepers, teachers,
   doctors, nurses,
   and all who work in this area.

O God, hear my prayer,
   and bless my life to your service.

## *May God's kingdom come*

229    Lord, in the stillness of your peace:

I pray for all those involved
    with missionary work
    both abroad and at home;
    that they may be protected
    from danger and disease,
    and led in the way of your will,
    so that their caring, forgiving lives
    witness to your love.

I pray for all the people of this earth
    who do not know you;
    for those who see you only as a threat
    or an excuse for violence;
    that they may be brought into contact
    with the living Christ
    who longs to give them his peace.

I pray for those in physical or mental pain;
    those weakened and exhausted by illness,
    those in intensive care
    or undergoing emergency surgery;
    that your healing power
    will sustain them
    and make them whole.

I pray for those with whom I live
    and work and worship;
    that we may use every opportunity
    to care for each other
    and grow in patience and understanding.
In Jesus' name I ask.

## Costly grace

Lord, I pray to you                                                   *230*
   on whom all things depend.

Encourage those whose Christian witness
   has brought embarrassment,
   rejection or persecution;
   that with their sights fixed on Jesus,
   they may be strengthened and encouraged,
   and remain his faithful friends.

Give grace to all negotiators, diplomats,
   envoys and advisers;
   that they may seek peace
   rather than war,
   unity rather than division,
   and justice
   rather than personal success.

May your healing love
   work within those
   who have been discouraged or hurt;
   all who harbour resentment
   and the desire for revenge;
   the lonely, the timid,
   the vulnerable and the abused.

Be known in this local community
   and all its homes, shops,
   schools, surgeries and leisure facilities;
   that Christ's life and brightness
   may infuse it with his love.
In his name I pray.

## *Praying to the Father*

231    As you have invited me to do,
        I pray to you, heavenly Father:

            for the continuous worship of the Church
            in every different climate, culture and season;
            that the waves of constant praise
            may never be broken;
            that Christians may pray attentively,
            joyfully and faithfully.

        For those in positions of authority;
            that they may neither abuse their power
            nor ignore their responsibilities
            but act with integrity, compassion
            and generosity of spirit.

        For all families split by political boundaries,
            war or natural disasters;
            all who have nowhere to call home;
            those for whom no one cares or prays.

        For my own family,
            for family life
            throughout the whole world;
            that all homes may be blessed
            with love and security
            and reflect your love for your children.

        God my Father,
            rejoicing in your tenderness and compassion,
            I bring these prayers before you
            through Jesus Christ my Lord.

## Good News of eternal life

Heavenly Father,                                                   *232*
   help me quieten myself and pray.

I pray for the Church,
   that having led others,
   Christians may not themselves
   be found wanting;
   that we may be open
   to what you call us to do.

Bring peace to this busy, rushed
   and anxious world;
   to those weighed down
   with responsibilities,
   and to the daily routine
   of millions of individuals
   on this earth;
   that each may know
   life in all its abundance.

Refresh those who profess to believe,
   but whose lives are dark and joyless;
   that they may experience the
   welcoming love of Christ
   and be drawn more fully
   into his resurrection life.

Give grace to me and my family;
   that we may not waste our life on earth
   pursuing futile goals,
   but commit ourselves absolutely
   to following Christ.
In his name I pray.

## Lord of peace

233   Lord of peace, quieten my heart
        to listen and to pray.

      I pray for all Christians
        involved in teaching and nursing,
        and those who have chosen
        to live simple lives;
        for the growth and development
        of a strong prayer life
        in each one.

      I pray for the world of industry
        and commerce;
        for those whose decisions
        affect many lives;
        for those who determine the use
        of our world's resources.

      I pray for those who are suffering
        from stress and depression;
        for those who cannot cope
        with the burdens of their lives;
        for psychiatric nursing staff
        and all carers.

      I pray for myself and my family;
        for a greater simplicity
        in the ordering of our lives;
        for deeper trust and acceptance.

      Heavenly Father,
        accept my prayers,
        through Jesus Christ my Lord.

## *Christ, the Saviour, is here*

In the presence of Christ, I pray:                                    *234*

    that the church may worship and adore
    faithfully and courageously
    in every age,
    coming to know Christ
    more and more;

    that the world may recognise
    and believe
    that Jesus is truly
    the Son of God;

    that all those in physical,
    mental, emotional or spiritual need
    may be comforted;

    that in celebrating my own faith
    I may be sensitive
    to others' needs,
    kind, helpful
    and full of gratitude.

Heavenly Father,
    accept these prayers
    and give me the strength and the will
    to walk in love,
    through Jesus Christ my Lord.

## *Facing hardship*

235    Loving heavenly Father,
          I approach you as your child
          with the needs and cares
          of your Church and your world:

          the problems of communications
          in the Church, and in all church groups;
          the difficulties of finding
          enough church leaders, cleaners,
          teachers, visitors
          to work effectively for you;

          the pressures on those in business
          to think only in terms of what is profitable;
          the problems of wealth distribution
          which cause such unnecessary suffering;

          the shortage of staff
          and resources in hospitals;
          the distress of those with no hospital at all;
          those who are in physical pain,
          mental anguish or spiritual darkness;

          the things that irritate,
          anger and frustrate me;
          the jobs that I find difficult to do cheerfully;
          the relationships I find demanding and tiring.

       Father, you are so generous;
          please fulfil my prayers
          in the way that is best for us all.
          I ask in the name of Jesus Christ.

## *Jesus is Lord in all circumstances*

Loving Father, I commend to you         *236*
  all who persist in working
  to spread the news
  of Christ's saving love
  in spite of poor conditions,
  hostility or danger.

I commend to you
  all who have been elected to govern
  both locally and internationally;
  that being guided by the light
  of truth and goodness
  they may be good stewards
  of the resources in their care.

I commend to you
  the chronically and critically ill,
  and those who tend them;
  the babies being born today,
  and the people who will die today.

I commend to you
  those we love who do not yet know Christ,
  or have turned away from him;
  that through circumstances
  and relationships
  they may be drawn to seek him.

Father of mercy,
  hear my prayers
  which I offer through Jesus Christ.

## *Obedience to Christ*

237    Lord, let me gather into your love
          all those for whom I pray:

             all who are working for Christian unity;
             that their work may be guided and blessed
             with integrity, wisdom and purity;

             all judges, and those serving on juries;
             those who make laws in this country
             and throughout the world;
             that our human laws may reflect
             your unchanging law and will
             made known to us in Christ;

             those whose minds have been poisoned
             by exposure to violence;
             children who have been abandoned
             or maltreated;
             all who crave affection
             but are frightened
             to become emotionally involved
             in case they get hurt.

             my own areas of weakness;
             that I may be remade by your grace
             into the person you desire me to be.

        Heavenly Father,
             in your love and mercy hear my prayers,
             through Jesus Christ.

## The challenge of faith

United in your Spirit with all faithful people,    *238*
   I pray to you, heavenly Father:

   that Christians may proclaim the full truth
   about Jesus Christ,
   without dilution or distortion,
   even though that truth
   may sometimes be unpalatable;

   that we may be wise and careful stewards
   of the resources of our world,
   so as to live out our thankfulness;

   that those who are physically hungry
   may be fed;
   and those who hunger and thirst
   for real meaning in life
   may be led to find lasting nourishment
   in Jesus;

   that having received Christ
   into my heart,
   I may joyfully,
   in words and actions,
   spread the marvellous news of his saving love.

Father,
   I can never thank you enough
   for what you have done for me,
   and for the way you are transforming lives.
With grateful heart, I offer you these prayers
   in the name of Jesus.

## *Working for God's glory*

239    Father, I come to you
        as a child you love.

    I bring to your love
        those whose Christian ministry
        is in prisons, hospitals, schools or industry;
        those who work among the homeless
        and the very poor.

    I bring to your love
        areas of political tension and unrest;
        the unresolved conflicts
        and the deep-seated grudges
        that hinder peace.

    I bring to your love
        the hurt and wounded,
        the abused and the frightened;
        women in labour and newly born babies;
        those who are approaching death.

    I bring to your love the needs
        of those who live or work in this area,
        and any who have particularly
        asked for my prayers.
        *[mention these by name]*

    With special joy, Father, in the knowledge
        that you love us unconditionally,
        I offer you these prayers,
        through Jesus Christ.

## Trust God and fear not

To you, Lord and heavenly Father,         *240*
   I bring my prayers in the name of Christ.

I pray that the spiritual life
   of each church community
   may be nurtured and grow,
   to reach out increasingly
   to the particular needs
   of the neighbourhood.

I pray that your will may prevail
   in the way we use our world's resources,
   our intelligence, our knowledge
   and our power.

I pray that all those
   who are living through some tempest,
   whether physical, emotional,
   mental or spiritual,
   may know the peace and comfort
   of your absorbent love
   which soaks up all hurt
   and promotes healing and wholeness.

I pray that my home may be a haven
   of caring and understanding,
   where all who enter may find
   your tangible and attractive peace.

Father, rejoicing that you are
   in overall charge of all creation,
   I offer these prayers
   through Jesus Christ.

## *Rooted in Christ*

241    Loving God, I ask you to deepen
        the personal commitment
        of every Christian,
        so that the life-giving sap
        of Christ the true vine
        can flood through the church
        and out into the world.

Direct and further
    all international discussions
    so that they lead to peace,
    goodwill and greater understanding.

Bring healing to those who are ill,
    peace to the anxious,
    courage to the fearful
    and rest to the weary.

Lord, make your home in me,
    in my family and my home,
    my place of work
    and in my local community,
    so that all our characters can be forged
    by your Spirit in us.

Merciful Father,
    fulfil my needs
    and those of your world
    according to your loving wisdom,
    through Jesus Christ.

## The light of Christ is revealed

Loving God, hear my prayer           *242*
   for the Church and for the world.

I pray that all Christian witness
   in a confused and nervous world
   may shine with a piercing integrity
   and warmth
   that awakens people's hearts
   to the love of you, their creator.

I pray that all travellers and pilgrims
   may be blessed and protected;
   that we may learn to cherish the beauty
   of our world
   and share its riches.

I pray that you will reveal
   the best practical ways
   of providing shelter for the homeless,
   safe accommodation for those
   who live in fear of violence,
   and food for the hungry.

I pray that I may learn to see Christ
   in the eyes of all those I meet,
   and delight in giving you glory
   by serving others
   without expecting rewards.

In thankfulness, Father,
   I offer you my life and my prayers,
   through Jesus Christ.

# Index